# Children at the Table

## THE COMMUNION
## OF ALL THE BAPTIZED
## IN ANGLICANISM TODAY

Ruth A. Meyers, Editor,
for the Standing Liturgical Commission

The Church Hymnal Corporation, New York

# Contents

# Introduction

In the most recent prayer book revisions by churches of the Anglican Communion, the rites of Christian initiation have been subject to careful scrutiny and, in many churches, substantial revision. Variations in the traditional Anglican pattern—baptism, confirmation, admission to communion—were encouraged by Resolution 25 of the 1968 Lambeth Conference:

> The Conference recommends that each province or regional church be asked to explore the theology of baptism and confirmation in relation to the need to commission the laity for their task in the world, and to experiment in this regard.

This resolution was influenced by contemporary pastoral concerns and by the advance of liturgical scholarship, discussions which have continued in the twenty-five years since the conference.

Subsequent to the 1968 Lambeth Conference, some Anglican churches, notably those in New Zealand, the United States, and Canada, began to permit baptized but unconfirmed children to receive communion. The matter was discussed in other provinces, but the pace of change was slow. The Church of England and the Anglican Church of Australia planned to address the issue at their respective General Synods in 1985.

These factors prompted a group of liturgists to convene an international Anglican consultation, at Boston, Massachusetts, in 1985, to confer on the subject of children and communion. The participants prepared papers in advance, and the discussion at the Consultation led to a statement with recommendations to churches of the Anglican Communion. The "Boston Statement" and some of the papers were subsequently published as Grove Liturgical Study 44, edited by Colin Buchanan (*Nurturing Children in Communion* [Bramcote, Nott.: Grove Books, 1985]). This useful volume provided theological and historical documentation in addition to reports from several provinces of the Anglican Communion.

That Grove Liturgical Study is now out of print, although the findings of the Boston Consultation were reaffirmed by the Fourth International Anglican Liturgical Consultation, in Toronto, Canada, in 1991. Recognizing that the proceedings of the Boston Consultation continue to be pertinent, the Standing Liturgical Commission of the Episcopal Church invited me to edit an updated collection of essays. In addition to the essays contained in the original Grove Liturgical Study, this collection includes three additional papers from the Consultation and, in a separate section, three subsequent articles arising from continued discussion in the Episcopal Church (U.S.A.).

The varied nature of the materials and the number of years elapsed since the original publication have resulted in differing styles of essays in this volume. In some cases the articles have been updated, while others remain as they were first presented or published. Furthermore, the collection represents some of the diversity of views in Anglicanism today. For example, the English Evangelical Colin Buchanan criticizes the baptismal rite of the Episcopal Church because he views it as a two-stage rite of water and anointing. In contrast, Leonel Mitchell, a member of the committee which drafted the American rite, identifies several possible interpretations of the post-baptismal consignation with optional anointing and states his position that the consignation is integral to the celebration of baptism although not absolutely necessary.

These differing viewpoints notwithstanding, the Boston Consultation reached substantial agreement on the issue of children and communion as well as broader questions of Christian initiation. Understanding baptism as the sacramental sign of full incorporation into the church, the Consultation recommended that all baptized persons be admitted to communion. The essays in this volume reflect that basic agreement.

I extend my appreciation to the authors for their willingness to review their work and grant permission for republication of their essays. I also wish to express my gratitude to the original publishers of each essay for their permission to reissue the articles, sometimes in edited form.

The materials from the Boston Consultation are introduced with a new essay by Colin Buchanan, editor of the original publication, *Nurturing Children in Communion*. "Children and the Eucharist in the Tradition of the Church," by David Holeton, was written for the collection, *Nurturing Children in Communion*, and is reprinted with permission of the author. "Communion of All the Baptized and Anglican Tradition," by David Holeton, presented at the Boston Consultation and published in *Anglican Theological Review* 69 (1987):13-28, is reprinted with permission of the editor of *ATR*. "A Theological Reflection on the Experience of Inclusion/Exclusion at the Eucharist," by Kenneth Stevenson, presented at the Boston Consultation, was published first in *ATR* 68 (1986):212-21 and later by The Pastoral Press in a collection of Stevenson's essays, *Worship: Wonderful and Sacred Mystery* (1992). It is reprinted here with permission of The Pastoral Press and the editor of *ATR*. "American Perspectives: (i) The Place of Baptismal Anointing," by Leonel Mitchell, presented at the Boston Consultation and published as "The Place of Baptismal Anointing in Christian Initiation" in *ATR* 68 (1986):202-11, is reprinted here with permission of the editor of *ATR*. "American Perspectives: (ii) Confirmation," by Louis Weil, was published in *Nurturing Children in Communion* and is reprinted in amended form with permission of the author. "American Perspectives: (iii) Mystagogia," by Robert Brooks, was published in *Nurturing Children in Communion* and is reprinted with permission of the author. "New Zealand Initiation Experience: (i) A Changing Initiatory Pattern," by Brian Davis, was published in *Nurturing*

*Children in Communion* and is reprinted in amended form with permission of the author. "New Zealand Initiation Experience: (ii) Acceptance of Child Communion," by Brian Davis and Tom Brown, was originally prepared for the 1991 International Anglican Liturgical Consultation and published as "Child Communion: How It Happened in New Zealand" in the collection of essays from that consultation, *Growing in Newness of Life* (Anglican Book Centre, 1993), edited by David Holeton. It is reprinted in amended form with permission of Anglican Book Centre. "Pushing at the Door: (i) The Church of England," by Donald Gray, published in *Nurturing Children in Communion*, has been substantially revised and updated and is printed here with permission of the author. "Pushing at the Door: (ii) The Anglican Church of Australia," by Ronald Dowling, was published in *Nurturing Children in Communion* and is reprinted with permission of the author. The addendum was newly written for this collection. "Ecumenical Perspectives," by Eugene Brand, presented at the Boston Consultation and included in abbreviated form in *Nurturing Children in Communion*, is printed here with permission of the author. The Boston Statement, "Children and Communion," was published in *Nurturing Children in Communion* and is reprinted here with permission of the Secretary-General of the Anglican Communion. (Unless otherwise noted above, all of the materials which appeared in *Nurturing Children in Communion* were originally presented to the Boston Consultation.)

"Infant Communion: Reflections on the Case from Tradition," by Ruth Meyers, is reprinted with permission from *Anglican and Episcopal History/The Historical Magazine of the Protestant Episcopal Church*, vol. LVII, No. 2, June 1988, pp. 159-175. "The Communion of Infants and Little Children," by Leonel Mitchell, was published in *ATR* 71 (1989):63-78 and is reprinted here with permission of the editor of *ATR*. "Disputed Aspects of Infant Communion," by Louis Weil, was published in *Studia Liturgica* 17

(1987):256-63 and is printed in amended form with permission of the editor of *Studia Liturgica.*

Appendix 1, "Communion of the Baptized but Unconfirmed," includes both the report of Paul Gibson, Coordinator for Liturgy, to the Joint Meeting of Primates and the Anglican Consultative Council in Cape Town, South Africa, January 1993, and more detail of the responses from some of the provinces of the Anglican Communion. Appendix 2 contains a statement of the mind of the House of Bishops of the Episcopal Church approved at the General Convention in July 1988.

This collection is offered in the hope that it will be of continuing use as provinces consider their theology and practice of admission to communion in light of renewed understandings of Christian initiation.

Ruth A. Meyers
Tuesday in Holy Week, 1994

# Contributors

Eugene L. Brand is Assistant General Secretary for Ecumenical Affairs, The Lutheran World Federation, Geneva, Switzerland.

Robert J. Brooks is The Presiding Bishop's Staff Officer for Washington, in the Washington (D.C.) Office of the Episcopal Church.

Tom Brown is Assistant Bishop of Wellington, New Zealand.

Colin Buchanan is Vicar of St. Mark's, Gillingham, and an Assistant Bishop of Rochester in the Church of England.

Brian Davis is Bishop of Wellington and Primate of the Province of Aotearoa, New Zealand, and Polynesia.

Ronald L. Dowling is Rector of the Church of St. Mary the Virgin, South Perth, Australia.

Donald Gray is a Canon of Westminster and a former Chair of the International Anglican Liturgical Consultation.

David R. Holeton is Dean of Divinity and Professor of Liturgics at Trinity College, Toronto, and current Chair of the International Anglican Liturgical Consultation.

Ruth A. Meyers is Diocesan Liturgist in the Diocese of Western Michigan and an Associate Faculty Member, Ecumenical Theological Seminary, Detroit, Michigan.

Leonel L. Mitchell is Professor of Liturgics at Seabury-Western Theological Seminary, Evanston, Illinois.

Kenneth W. Stevenson is Rector of Holy Trinity and St. Mary's, Guildford.

Louis Weil is Professor of Liturgics at Church Divinity School of the Pacific, Berkeley, California.

# The Boston Consultation
# on Children at Communion

# The Boston Consultation:
# A New Introduction to the Essays

*Colin Buchanan*

It is a joy to know of the projected republication of the essays and statement that sprang from the Boston International Anglican Liturgical Consultation in July 1985. It might of course be argued that the fifteen participants who made up the Consultation were neither fully representative of the Anglican Communion geographically and culturally, nor were even the best liturgical and sacramental scholars available to fulfill a demanding path-finding task for the Communion. Nevertheless, even if that is conceded—and it would only be allowed reluctantly—yet the theme of "Children and Communion" was insistent from many parts of the world, the need to tackle it internationally was obvious, and the fifteen persons together were no mean theological agency to point the way ahead.

Irrespective of the actual subject considered, the Consultation by its sheer existence was a trailblazing exercise in the Anglican Communion. There had been pan-Anglican Consultations on liturgy before, but they had been "once-offs" consisting of certain persons in Toronto for the pan-Anglican Congress in 1963 and certain others in London for the Lambeth Conference in 1968. But at Boston in 1985 a pan-Anglican institution with a continuity of life began, privately inspired in the first instance, but to be adopted by the Anglican Consultative Council (ACC) in the years 1987 to 1990, and to be further recognized by the Primates and the ACC at the Cape Town, South Africa, meeting in January 1993. This first Consultation originated through the initiative of David Holeton, then Professor at Vancouver School of Ministry; and he, acting as secretary, in conjunction with Donald Gray, Canon of Westminster Abbey in London (who became chairman), convened the Boston gathering and began the sequence of "International Anglican Liturgical Consultations (IALCs)."

For reasons of financial and travelling convenience the first four Consultations were held in conjunction with the biennial Congress of Societas Liturgica, the international, interdenominational association of Christian liturgists. These were held: at Boston, USA, in July 1985; at Brixen, northern Italy, in August 1987; at York, England, in August 1989; and at Toronto, Canada, in August 1991.[1] It was from the second of these that the request for official recognition came, and it was at the third that the role of the ACC in giving it official standing within the Communion was fulfilled. In principle this meant that the ACC, whilst it was unlikely to provide much financial help, could advise on the agenda, appoint a link person from their membership to serve on the IALC steering committee, and provide a place of accountability and resource for the IALC.

Such was the Anglican institution being launched at Boston. But at that first IALC the interest lay in its own theme, children and communion. The subject chosen no doubt reflected the interests and perceptions of the convenors themselves, but clearly also echoed the actual immediate agenda in many parts of the Communion. It was also significant that it was *liturgists* who were handling the topic, as the conventional wisdom of Anglicanism seemed to be that decisions relating to admission to communion are pastoral, disciplinary or canonical ones—stemming from bishops, synods, or canon lawyers—and are only peripherally the concern of liturgists. In their choice of this subject, the liturgists were quietly asserting their freedom from a straitjacketed concentration on solely verbal jigsaws. This distortion of their task is a cartoon role which is often wished or fastened upon liturgists by others (which then brings a consequent distrust or downgrading of the whole world of liturgy), but it is in fact a serious misreading of their calling, their subject matter, and their contribution to the equipping and renewing of Christ's church. Liturgy is full-orbed *event*, in which the participants are as important as the program— and the liturgical life is life marked by an ordered sequence of such full-orbed *events*. The application of this principle to initiatory events is obvious—the liturgist is concerned for not only the baptismal *text*, but also the baptismal *candidates* (including their age, qualifications, preparation, and participation), and the baptismal *celebration* (including the time of year and of day; the architectural, sociological and liturgical context; the choreography, decor and leadership; and the involvement of sponsors, witnesses and other assistants). It was this kind of full-orbed understanding of liturgy which at Boston gathered the liturgists to consider, and consider as a function of sacramental initiation, the issue of children and communion.

Interestingly, there was one person present who did come much more as a pastor, without having been previously known in academic liturgical circles. That one was Brian Davis from New Zealand, then Bishop of Waikato, but now Bishop of Wellington and Archbishop of the (newly renamed) Province of Aotearoa, New Zealand and Polynesia. He was already known to a number of people beyond New Zealand as the pioneer of the admission of unconfirmed children to communion within the Anglican Communion—a practice he had pioneered as a father of a young family when he was Dean of Waiapu in the late 1960s, which led into the story he tells (without mention of his own role) as "New Zealand Initiation Experience" below. This had given the Province of New Zealand (as it then was) a head start in the Anglican Communion. As I wrote in the 1985 Introduction:

> there is occasion to salute two notable pioneers, who
> met each other for the first time at Boston, and
> between them provide more than one-third of the total

new material in this study. I refer of course to Brian Davis and David Holeton—the practical reformer from New Zealand, and the rigorous (but very charming) theologian of the reform from Canada...the essayists join together in saluting these trailblazers, to whom Anglicans of the future owe much.[2]

At the Boston Consultation the liturgists found themselves all pulling at the same end of the rope. The statement took shape without any sense of major theological discord, despite a considerable spread of churchmanship and of geographical provenance.[3] Undergirding the whole process there were very clear agreed convictions:

**a** Sacramental initiation is, *qua* outward administration of the initiatory sign, complete in water-baptism;

**b** Water-baptism is appropriately given to the infants of believing Christians;

**c** Baptism, whenever it is given, is itself the gateway for admission to participation in the eucharist.

The nearest to a deviation from this consensus that could be detected lay in the contemporary American practice. It was not that children could not be admitted to communion before confirmation in the Episcopal Church—quite the reverse, for the USA had come little behind New Zealand in that practice. It was rather that in that church baptism itself—even infant baptism—seemed to provide a two-stage ceremony of water and anointing. This led me to write in the 1985 Introduction:

> And, whilst the rites make it clear now that "Confirmation" belongs not with "initiation" but with "Pastoral Offices," yet the provision for anointing by the bishop at infant baptism reads remarkably like the "Eastern Orthodox" pattern, which contributors here deliberately eschew. The commentators on the American book do wallow slightly when they come to this point, and the Boston participants were

glad that the American signatories of the Statement could agree that "Any additional ceremonies [i.e., over and above the administration of water]....should not be seen as essential." All liturgists have, of course, sometimes to face the question, "What does it mean to say that something is rubrically requisite but should not 'be seen as essential'?" Is this to make a distinction without a difference? And if it is, then the American rites (no less than others elsewhere) may need not so much explication as alteration.[4]

Other countries varied. On the one hand New Zealand and Canada were ahead of the USA in implementing Boston principles. Indeed Canada, in its then newly authorized *Book of Alternative Services*, did not require anything that might rank as "confirmation" or a second stage of initiation within the rite of either an infant or an adult baptism—a cleaner liturgical outworking of the new pattern than any other province could show. Obviously those baptized as infants would still be expected to be confirmed if they grew up believing and communicant, but those baptized as adults were clearly fully initiated in water-baptism, and all other ceremonies were optional extras.

On the other hand, the Church of England, which had failed dismally to change its provisions for admission to communion in the years 1974-76,[5] was in 1985 making brave noises which proved all too soon to be frustrated. The "Knaresborough" Report, *Communion before Confirmation?*, had been completed before July 1985 and was provided to the Boston Consultation in duplicated form. In it the working party, of which I was myself a member, unanimously proposed the kind of pattern at which Boston itself arrived. In the process of compiling the report between 1982 and 1985 we had taken frequent soundings amongst the bishops, and although we knew of bishops who were hesitant about running ahead of changes in the law, we encountered relatively few who were opposed in principle. There were also dioceses where widespread pioneering (though illegal) projects[6] were being encour-

aged, or at least not discouraged, amongst the parishes. Any query-
ing there might be of these usually turned out to be based not on
legal grounds as such, nor on theological grounds (that the unconfirmed are not sufficiently initiated to be proper recipients of communion), but much more on the grounds that it is improper to
admit children to communion in one place if you cannot sustain
their admission in every place. So the Knaresborough Report went
from our hands to the General Synod with some confidence and
hope, and its text encouraged the Boston participants, whilst the
English at Boston had good hopes that the Boston Statement
might itself help the favorable wind that was apparently blowing in
England. The English story from then on proved a sad disappointment, as Donald Gray reports in his essay, "Pushing at the Door:
(i) The Church of England."

The next international Anglican attention to the issue came at
the Lambeth Conference in 1988. I was myself secretary of the
small group at that conference which worked on the renewal of
worship, and we brought drafts which raised the issue to our section on "Mission and Ministry," one of the four sections into
which the whole conference was divided. There a maverick bishop
or two jumped up, declared that confirmation was under attack,
and led sufficient bishops into opposing it on that basis to have the
drafting excised. Venturesomeness was not the name of the game,
and an observer might have been pardoned for thinking that
springing to defend confirmation at the merest allegation that it
was under threat was a kind of episcopal Pavlovian reflex.

At the Lambeth Conference itself, some of the ground was
regained. Brian Davis put in a private member's resolution:

> This Conference requests all Provinces to consider the
> theological and pastoral issues involved in the admis-
> sion of those baptized but unconfirmed to commu-
> nion (as set out in the Report of ACC-7), and to
> report their findings to the ACC.[7]

This was not opposed in the plenary sessions, so it was passed "on
the nod." It is not clear how far provinces of the Communion have

acted upon it, but it remains on record (admittedly without a deadline), and the ACC ought to be ready to prod individual provinces for a response.[8]

Within a few years, the issue of children and communion returned to the agenda of the International Anglican Liturgical Consultation. The IALCs were growing and involving people from larger and larger numbers of provinces. The 1989 York Statement on inculturation, entitled "Down to Earth Worship," had clearly had the whole Anglican Communion and its ways of worship in view.[9] Once it was clear that the Consultations were not simply trying to find a way of stating an agreed mind of the participants as a kind of given but static theological point of reference thereafter, but were actively trying to reform the life of the Communion, it was clear that initiation must come on the agenda again. For Africa, Asia, South America and the Caribbean had hardly been represented at Boston, but were now flexing creative muscles and were wanting to have participants at successive Consultations.

It was crucial that the widest constituency possible should look at the Boston issues again, and should look at them within the widest possible context of Christian initiation, rather than solely driven by the one issue. Thus it was that sixty-three liturgists from seventeen provinces of the Communion (including a dozen bishops) looked in depth at current initiation questions in the Anglican Communion at Toronto at IALC-4 in August 1991. At this Consultation, they reaffirmed the Boston findings but made a much longer statement of their own.[10] It is that statement, commended for study by the Primates and Anglican Consultative Council, which constitutes for some time the pressing agenda for both international and provincial Anglican exploration. What is clear, however, is that Toronto would not have been Toronto had Boston not stood behind it. This publication therefore returns Anglicans to recent historical roots in the latter-day quest for a radical but biblical Anglican pattern of Christian initiation.

# Notes

1. The fifth IALC is scheduled to accompany the Congress of Societas Liturgica at Dublin, Ireland, in August 1995. Preparatory work on the eucharist was done for that Consultation at an interim conference at Untermarchtal, Germany, in August 1993.

2. *Nurturing Children in Communion*, Grove Liturgical Study 44(Bramcote, Nott.: Grove Books, 1985), p. 6.

3. There was, it must be acknowledged, no proper representation of "third world" provinces in Africa, Asia or South America. This was the subject of a note in the text and an explanatory footnote in my 1985 Introduction. There has been from that date onwards an awareness in the successive IALCs that their findings must come from a true spectrum of the existent Anglican Communion.

4. Grove Liturgical Study 44, p. 6; the quotation begining "Any additional ceremonies..." is from the statement, II.C.1, below, p.134. The question is almost exactly the question of the Elizabethan and Stuart Puritans about the "excepted cere-monies"—*viz.*, if kneeling at communion, say, is not of com-mandment from God, then what is the church doing when it enforces its use?

5. Almost contemporaneously with the first moves in New Zealand and the USA, there was published in England in 1971 the "Ely Report," *Christian Initiation: Birth and Growth in the Christian Society* (CIO, 1971), which unanimously rec-ommended that children baptized but not yet confirmed should be admitted to communion. This was sent to the dio-ceses in 1974 with a complex pattern of questions to answer, and it came back with an equivocal reply, almost certainly traceable to the form of the questions. Hence no lawful action was taken in the Church of England in the 1970s, though projects, technically illegal, developed apace.

6. The term "experiments" is more commonly used to describe such projects (i.e., admission to communion before confirmation), but this term is often employed to help make the case for phasing out a project. After all, who could favor experimenting on children's religious lives? I prefer to call them "pioneering projects" and submit that this is a wholly reasonable and unemotive description.

7. Resolution 69, *The Truth Shall Make You Free*, p. 239.

8. Editor's note: see Appendix 1 for data from some provinces of the Anglican Communion.

9. See David Holeton, ed., *Liturgical Inculturation in the Anglican Communion*, Alcuin/GROW Joint Liturgical Study 15 (Bramcote, Nott.: Grove Books, 1990).

10. See David Holeton, ed., *Growing in Newness of Life: Christian Initiation in Anglicanism Today* (Toronto: Anglican Book Centre, 1993), for the papers and findings of the Fourth International Anglican Liturgical Consultation, Toronto 1991.

## 2

# Children and the Eucharist in the Tradition of the Church

*David R. Holeton*

More has been written in the past two decades about the nature and development of Christian initiation than in the entire previous history of the church. Three central themes have emerged: 1. the essential unity of the rite (baptism, confirmation and first communion belong together); 2. the "oneness" of the rite (the dichotomy between infant and adult baptism is a false dichotomy); 3. the context of the rite (Sunday morning within the celebration of the eucharist rather than Sunday afternoon in a "private" service). I should like to use these three themes as instruments with which to reassess the question of young children and the eucharist in Christian tradition.

## The Unity of Baptism

The celebration of new life in Jesus Christ is a rich and complex affair. One of the major benefits of the Lima statement on baptism (*Baptism, Eucharist and Ministry*, World Council of Churches, Faith and Order Paper 111) is its delineation of the richness of New Testament baptismal imagery. When we examine our own baptismal rites, however, and search for that variety of baptismal imagery, we quickly find our traditional rites to be wanting. This is by no means uniquely an Anglican problem. Our Western liturgical tradition as a whole has placed its primary emphasis on baptism as a washing away of sin and participation in the death of

Christ. In so doing, it has allowed other images—e.g., baptism as the anointing of the Spirit, baptism as incorporation into the eschatological community—to take on a secondary character.

In the early church, this richness of baptismal imagery was held in tension by the unity of the various actions of the rite. If you asked any church father whether baptism without the eucharist could constitute admission into the church, the answer would have been an unequivocal "No!" John 3.5 ("Unless one is born of water and the Spirit...") and John 6.53 ("Unless you eat the flesh of the Son of Man...") were the key biblical texts, used in the form of a couplet to underline the essential unity of baptism and the eucharist.

As the richness of baptismal imagery began to wane, however, the seeds were sown for the separation of the various components of the rite. In the early sixth century, a North African bishop, Fulgentius of Ruspe, was presented with a pastoral problem. A baptizand was reported to have died during the baptismal liturgy—after the water rite and anointing, but before the reception of communion. Was the person saved? Fulgentius replied in the affirmative—a pastoral answer to a pastoral question. Centuries later, when for practical reasons the anointing which came to be called confirmation was delayed until a bishop could visit the outlying portions of his diocese, and when first communion was delayed until after confirmation in order to force parents to present their children for confirmation, this text, now attributed to Augustine, came to be used as a theological proof-text to legitimize the separation of communion from baptism. The way was opened for denying children the eucharist.

## One Rite

The rise of Anabaptism in the sixteenth century presented the church with a dichotomy unknown in its previous history. Infant baptism and adult (believer's) baptism came to be seen as two separate realities. The polemic used by Pedobaptists on one side and

Anabaptists on the other only served to obscure the reality that the categories themselves were novelties and the dichotomy false. For Anglicans, this dichotomy was reinforced in 1662 when the Book of Common Prayer presented two baptismal rites—one to be used for children and a new rite to be used for those of "riper years." The introduction of this new rite unwittingly capitulated a principle which had been maintained since the beginning of documented Christian practice—that there is one rite of baptism, regardless of the age of the candidate.

The historical evidence overwhelmingly indicates that age was not a factor in determining who could be baptized. Hippolytus, Cyprian, Augustine, John the Deacon, the Gregorian Sacramentary, the Roman *Ordines*, all offer specific evidence for infants participating with adults in the baptismal action. As the unity of the baptismal rite itself was not in question at this time, infants who were baptized obviously received communion. All the baptized received the eucharist from the New Testament period onwards.

Until at least the thirteenth century almost all liturgical books prescribed that children be admitted to communion at baptism. Following their baptismal communion, infants and young children received communion frequently, in some places immediately after the clergy, in others, immediately after the adults. Even when the "private" administration of baptism came to replace its public celebration at the great festivals, infants continued to receive communion at baptism from the reserved sacrament, usually under the species of wine.

## The Context of the Celebration

The crucial issue for the admission of children to the eucharist is the relationship between the sacraments and the Christian community. Paul wrote: "The fact that there is only one loaf means that, though there are many of us, we form a single body because we all have a share in this one loaf" (1 Cor. 10.17). The eucharist was given for the life of the community as a whole. That the bread of life was meant for children also is attested to in the first miracle of the feeding of the multitude—there were "about five thousand men, besides women and children" (Mt. 14.21).

The daily breaking of bread which characterized the life of the first Christian communities (Acts 2.46), along with participation in the communities' acts of love (Acts 5.42; 6.1), took place in domestic rather than "ecclesiastical" settings. Where infants and little children were members of these households, they were undoubtedly included, participating in the common (eucharistic) meal. The baptism which was able to transcend distinctions of race, social status and gender (Gal. 3.28) was also capable of transcending distinctions of age! Indeed, both the New Testament and the tradition take the young very seriously. Children are held up as the ideal inheritors of the kingdom (of which the eucharist is a foretaste), while those who were new in the faith were called, regardless of age, *infantes.*

For the patristic church, it was baptism *and* eucharist which established membership in the Christian community. Membership thereafter depended on continued participation in the eucharist. For Cyprian, to abandon the eucharist was to abandon the church, which was to abandon Christ. Cyprian repeatedly made it clear that this is true regardless of age. Augustine made the point in a different way when he said: "You are the body of Christ and its members; it is your own mystery which lies there on the Lord's Table. It is your own mystery which you receive. It is to what you are that you respond 'Amen'" (*Sermon* 272). As long as the regular reception of the eucharist was seen as a constitutive act of ongoing membership in the body of Christ, no question was ever raised as to the appropriateness of all the baptized receiving the eucharistic body.

But this understanding began to weaken. The seeds for the divorce between eucharist and community were inadvertently sown by some of the great pastoral bishops in the fourth century

(John/Cyril? of Jerusalem, Ambrose, Theodore of Mopsuestia, John Chrysostom). When faced with the massive influx of new Christians, these bishops attempted to heighten the sense of *mysterium tremendum* surrounding the eucharist, often using awesome images not unlike those of the old mystery religions. Thus Isidore of Seville could write of God literally descending from heaven during the Canon (*Etymologiae* VI, 38.)

The process of separation between eucharist and community was reinforced by the Arian crisis. A major sacramental reaction to Arianism was an increased emphasis on the adoration of the divinity present in the eucharistic species. This adoration cultivated a devotion which fostered eucharistic abstinence out of respect for the eucharistic elements themselves. Eventually criteria would be introduced for communicant status which involved qualities associated with attaining the age of reason (recognition, devotion, discretion, confession).

This increasing eucharistic abstinence was further exacerbated by the growing effects of established Christianity. Before the Peace of the Church (c. 315), and for at least the century which followed, it was reception of the eucharist on Sunday which constituted the affirmation that the individual was, and wished to remain, a member of the church. It is only in this context that we can understand the importance placed on the sacrament being taken to the sick and to those imprisoned for their faith.

But establishment changed all that. Reception of the eucharist on Sundays ceased to be the sign of continued participation in the body. Simply living in a now-Christian society took its place. The richness evoked when one mentioned the body of Christ (Christ risen, ascended, glorified; the company of all the faithful; the eucharistic body) disappeared. A gulf developed between the *Corpus Mysticum* (the church) and the *Corpus Verum* (the eucharistic body). The only concern remaining was that both baptism and the eucharist must be received *for salvation*, rather than as a dimension of continuing life within the Christian community. Even this vestigial practice gradually disappeared after the twelfth century (largely because of the disappearance of the lay chalice), leaving scholastic theologians in the difficult position of explaining how both baptism and the eucharist are necessary for salvation and how the baptized infant had a right to the eucharist but did not actually receive the physical elements (cf. Thomas Aquinas, *Super Mat.* 6.3).

Increasingly, then, the laity became spectators rather than participators at the eucharist. By the time the laity stopped receiving the cup and baptismal communion disappeared, there was so little sense that baptism admitted to the eucharistic fellowship that the practice of baptismal communion disappeared almost without protest. Private baptism could become normative in the Anglican tradition and children could be denied access to the table, because neither baptism nor eucharist had been essentially associated with the ongoing life of the Christian community.

### New Directions

What do these historical reflections have to say to our own situation? Resolution 25 of Lambeth 1968 pushed Anglican provinces into a serious theological examination of Christian initiation. The theological reports which emerged weighed heavily on the side of a reunified rite of baptism. Contemporary historical research on the development of baptismal practice played an important role in the formation of those reports. Pastoral reflection on the increasing difficulties with the traditional pattern of initiation (baptism on demand without ongoing contact with the church; confirmation as graduation from both religious education *and* church) further delineated problems inherent in a divided rite.

The result of this would seem to be a theological and historical consensus that the unity of the baptismal rite ought to be restored. Certainly the ecumenical consensus (at least on paper) is that baptism admits to the eucharist. This datum is being taken seriously and is beginning to have an effect on some of the new baptismal liturgies appearing in various provinces.

As these rites appear, several important elements emerge. There is a gradual movement to having one baptismal rite for both adults and children. This effectively ends the false dichotomy between infant and adult (believer's) baptism. The inherent "oneness" of the rite is being made explicit. The sealing/imposition of hands, as one of the rites which helps explicate the symbolic richness of the baptismal event, is being restored to a more visible place in the new liturgical material.

Most important, however, is the context in which the celebration of baptism is taking place. It is both public and eucharistic. Anglican communities increasingly are coming to recognize that baptism has a great deal to do with participation in the life of a very specific Christian community. Baptism has ceased to be an event which affects only a family and close friends, and has become an event which affects the lives of each member of the community. Sometimes we do not take our own liturgical texts sufficiently seriously. The question addressed to the whole congregation which has appeared in a number of our new rites and which asks: "Will you do everything in your power to support and uphold these persons in their new life in Christ?" has proved a locus from which the congregation's role and responsibility in Christian nurture is being taken with a fresh seriousness. A few congregations (laity, not clergy) are beginning to demand some sign of commitment to the Christian life from baptismal families. The restoration of baptism as an act of public worship has revolutionary implications.

The rubric which directs that baptism take place in the context of the eucharist has implications which are even more revolutionary, however. Revolutionary because this century has witnessed a revolution in Anglican eucharistic piety and practice. The gradual emergence of the eucharist as the principal act of worship on the Lord's Day has realized the hopes of the Reformers and brought us back in touch with our Christian origins. But perhaps as important as the restored Sunday eucharist is the growing sense, among many Anglicans, that the weekly reception of communion is a constitutive act both in their own lives and in the life of the Christian community to which they belong. These communities themselves are increasingly diverse and much more faithfully reflect the social community in which they are located (racially, socially and in age).

To celebrate baptism in the context of a renewed eucharistic community—one which sees the eucharist as constitutive of its very life—begins to have serious implications. The primary implication is contained in the question: "Should not all members of the community share in the bread which gives the community life?" The only answer we can draw from looking at the Christian tradition is: "But of course!"

To come to that conclusion is not novel. If we look at the experience of churches whose lives were lived long after the patristic period, lives characterized by a strong sense of community and a high value placed on the Sunday eucharist, we will find a major emphasis on the communion of all the baptized. These Christians—Bohemians, Nonjurors, Catholic Apostolics—all had a passionate feeling for the vitality of community life in the early church, a vitality which they wished to experience in their own time. It was a vitality which they saw rooted in the common sharing by all the baptized in the Bread of Life. The conclusion to which they came, often looking at basically the same evidence Anglicans have studied for the past twenty years, is slowly becoming our own.

# 3

# Communion of All the Baptized and Anglican Tradition

*David R. Holeton*

## Introduction

Almost thirty years after Lambeth 1968 took a major initiative in pushing the Anglican Communion towards the reform of its pattern of Christian initiation,[1] the idea of communicating all the baptized, infants included, is still being treated by many as a novel idea within Anglicanism and, as such, a practice that is foreign to Anglican thought.[2] Most of us seem to have taken the "traditional" practice of baptism, confirmation, and first communion as normative for the whole of Anglican history, forgetting that the faithful observance of this sequence is an innovation of the strict churchmanship of the nineteenth century and that, until the first quarter of that century, most communicant Anglicans were never confirmed.[3] In that context, it may be helpful to look at where the larger question of communicating all the baptized fits into the history of Anglican sacramental thought.

## Sixteenth-Century Origins

Discussion of the possibility of communicating infants and young children is almost as old as English Reformation literature itself. Thomas Cartwright, Lady Margaret Professor of Divinity at Cambridge and an early advocate of radical reform, raised the question as early as 1572.[4] Over the ensuing fifty years the question surfaced with increasing frequency. Thomas Morton (1564-1659), Bishop of Coventry and Lichfield and later Durham, raised the question,[5] as did William Ames, a radical (but conforming) Puritan.[6]

For each of these writers the question was raised for polemical reasons rather than as part of an attempt to restore the practice in the English church. Cartwright invokes the practice as the logical but, in his opinion, false consequence of Augustine's assertion that baptism is necessary for salvation. Morton, in an anti-Roman polemic, cites the patristic practice of infant communion to similar ends, arguing that if patristic witnesses for infant baptism as necessary for salvation are to be taken seriously, so too must similar witness to infant communion. If we are to accept the one, so must we accept the other. Ames uses the patristic evidence for infant communion as just one more piece of evidence in his treatise against liturgical ceremonies.

While each of these three witnesses to the communion of all the baptized is interested in polemic rather than restoration, the importance of their work cannot be dismissed. The coming years were to see these seeds sprout and flourish. That, however, was to depend on even more violent polemic.

The accusation that the English church was only half-reformed was well founded. The early English reformers (it is too early to call them Anglicans) found themselves in an embarrassing position. The reforms implied by their theological position far outstretched the length to which they could carry any reform of popular piety. Theologians like John Whitgift, who were entrusted with defending the English church against the attacks of more radical reformers, found themselves in the embarrassing position of being in essential agreement with their opponents in matters of sacramental theology but of having to present an apology for sacramental practice that was basically unchanged from that of the pre-Reformation medieval church. While, for example, both the prayer book and the English reformers held that baptism and eucharist were public acts essentially constitutive of the church, the pastoral reality was that private baptism (often administered domestically by midwives) remained usual, and only a handful of the faithful remained behind for the weekly eucharist when Matins and the Litany were over. A half-reformed church such as this was not the fertile ground required for any major reformation of sacramental practice, particularly in the sequence of Christian initiation.[7]

Reforming an established church is a painfully slow prospect, particularly when there is neither charismatic leadership nor a pressing sense of the eschatological moment. The English Reformation had little of either. As a result, any movement in the direction of serious reform of sacramental practice had to await the acrimonious theological debate on the eve of, and during, the Commonwealth. Here, in a new political context, Anglican sacramental theology achieved a clarity previously unattained, the consequences of which are much more profound than those of the previous century.

## Seventeenth-Century Debate

Perhaps unlike any previous age, the mid-seventeenth century was an age of print, and particularly an age of the pamphlet. Papers on every subject poured from the press and were devoured with interest by a readership much taken by popularized debate seasoned with liberal doses of calumny and vitriol. Theological topics were among the most popular for this sort of treatment. As England moved towards Civil War, Commonwealth, and Restoration, baptism became one of the theological topics most often debated. Radical dissent had come to have such strength that pedobaptism was being called into serious question. It was in the context of this debate that Anglican baptismal theology was subjected to a self-examination and clarification that had heretofore been unnecessary.

For two decades, beginning in 1641, the development of the baptismal debate can be traced in great detail thanks to the contemporary London bookseller, George Thomason, who collected and dated almost 15,000 pamphlets published during that period. From its inception, pedobaptists found themselves set against Baptists, some Puritans, and (after 1652) the Quakers. From the very beginning of the debate, the opponents of pedobaptism questioned pedobaptists' theological consistency in admitting infants to baptism but not to the eucharist. Edward Barber, a Baptist who was imprisoned in the Tower for denying infant baptism, put it this way:

> Whereas it is objected, children are of the Kingdom of God and have right to all the Ordinances, as so to Dipping. This consequence necessarily follows, that they have right also to the Lords Supper as well as Dipping, seeing right to all.[8]

The question, once posed, pushed pedobaptist theologians down two quite distinct paths. The first involved an examination of the relationship between the two sacraments and called into question the received sacramental model itself. The second involved an examination of the requirements that need be met before one was able to receive the sacraments, capacity and faith becoming the two principal instruments of analysis.

The attempt to make clear-cut distinctions between baptism and eucharist ran into trouble very quickly. This was, in part, a product of the contemporary sacramental theology in which Calvin's understanding of "sacrament as seal of the covenant" had achieved hegemony. If sacraments were primarily seals of the covenant, and essentially two forms of the same seal, it became awkward to explain how infants could receive one and not the other. Arguments to maintain the distinction between the two sacraments depended heavily on a biological model of the sacraments, which had emerged as one of the most popular sacramental paradigms in medieval theology.[9] In the context of medieval christendom, baptism had come to be related more to birth than to new birth; the eucharist had become related to growth, not in the sense of nourishment for growth but rather in the sense that a level of maturity was necessary before nourishment could take place. For baptism the passive qualities of infancy were required; for the eucharist the active qualities of maturity (taking, eating, remembering) were required.

This commonly received, but apparently unexamined, sacramental model broke down quite quickly when subjected to the attack of those upholding believer's baptism. This is well illustrated in a tract of John Tombes, one of the most inexhaustible opponents of infant baptism:

> In answer to the Objection, infants by the like reason should have the Lords Supper [the pedobaptist John Church] tells us "that the ceremonies are different, in the one the person is to be active, in the other passive": but the Scripture says it not so, but requires Baptism as a duty, and thereto profession of faith as a prerequisite. He saith, "Baptism is the Sacrament of entrance into the church, the other of progress"; but this proves the rather that infants should have the Lords Supper; fith [sic] they are to grow and make progress after their entrance. What he saith, "it cannot be given to infants," is false: for they can take Bread and Wine, and it was given them six hundred years together, as many both Protestants and Papists confess.[10]

The speed with which the biological model was abandoned is an interesting comment on the unexamined assumptions of English pedobaptist theology. A sacramental model, based on medieval pastoral practice, which assumed infants as the normative baptismal candidates, had been adopted uncritically. As soon as the model was subjected to sustained criticism it quickly became evident that it could not bear the weight of any examination founded on scripture, tradition, or even logical consistency. Baptism in the New Testament is no more about passivity than is the eucharist about activity. That infants received the eucharist in the early church had been commonly conceded since the early days of the English Reformation. The logical inconsistency in the biological model of the sacraments could not be rationalized without irreparably damaging the model itself. These three flaws in the argument were too much for pedobaptists. The biological model fell into desuetude as an argument against the admission of young children to the eucharist. Instead, those who continued to need a rationale for children's exclusion from the eucharistic meal turned to more specifically theological arguments: capacity and faith.

The categories of capacity and faith certainly were not new to the theological debate of the time. They were of primary concern in the ongoing baptismal debate. Whether or not infants were capable of faith, and if so, what sort of faith, were major questions posed to pedobaptists. To have admitted that infants were incapable of faith would have eviscerated a principal case for their baptism. But as soon as pedobaptists admitted that infants were capable of faith, the question was again posed: "Why not admit them to the eucharist?"

When the question was put, pedobaptists were quick to admit that infants are capable of faith. Some followed the line of positive agnosticism expressed by Calvin, who, when asked whether infants were capable of faith, replied, "We do not know that they are not." Others, like Thomas Fuller, came to a similar conclusion by a different route:

> They that have some degree of faith ought to be Baptised, but Infants have some degree of faith. The proof: "without faith it is impossible to please God" Heb. 11:6. But infants please God, therefore they have faith.[11]

The admission that children were capable of faith led some pedobaptists to make distinctions between types of faith: was the faith of infants common faith or was it justifying faith? Such sophistry ultimately bore little fruit. Even the indefatigable

Richard Baxter had to admit that "the Church hath ever from the Apostles daies till now, without question, admitted the new baptised, at age to the Lord's Supper, without requiring any new species of faith to entitle them to it."[12]

While objections to children's admission to the eucharist on grounds of lack of faith slowly withered, their capability on other grounds continued to be challenged. The most frequent objection used was the argument that infants are incapable of conforming to Paul's exhortation to self-examination (1 Cor. 11.28). Here the pedobaptists put themselves at the mercy of their opponents. If children were incapable of the biblical injunction to self-examination, and thus were to be excluded from the eucharist, so too were they incapable of the injunction to "repent and be baptized" (Acts 2.38), and thus ought to be excluded from baptism. Pedobaptists, it was argued, had to admit either that the church which could overlook one text could also overlook the other, where children were concerned, or else that both texts ought to be taken with equal seriousness, and children accordingly be excluded from baptism.

Henry Haggar argued the case this way:

> If all that are members of the body, do partake of that bread, and they that do partake of it must examine themselves, and so eat, then little infants that can neither speak nor understand, are no members visible of Christ's body the Church: for they can neither examine themselves, nor none else for them, because they cannot speak nor make answer.

> But all that are members of the body, do partake of the body, do partake of the one bread, 1 Cor. 10:17 and all that do partake of it, must examine themselves, and so eat of that bread &c.

> Therefore no such infants are visible members of Christ's body, which is the Church.[13]

Pedobaptists found themselves placed in a position that had

become untenable theologically. They could not admit that infants are incapable of baptism and incorporation into the body of Christ, yet they were unwilling to admit that they are capable of admission to the eucharist even though it is they, and not the anti-pedobaptists, who have clearly delineated the field of battle. It is Richard Baxter, one of the strongest advocates of infant baptism, who effectively admits defeat on the question of excluding infants from the eucharist for want of faith or other capacity. Having dealt with the traditional objections against infant baptism, he tried to turn the tables, requiring that his opponents prove to him that infants be admitted to the eucharist:

> I have fully proved that Infants must be baptised; Let them prove that they must receive the Lords Supper if they can: If they can bring as good proof for this, as I have done for the former, I shall heartily yield that they ought to receive both: Till then it lies on them and not on me; they that affirm that Infants should have the Lords Supper, must prove it; they cannot expect that I should prove the negative.[14]

This is a challenge which the anti-pedobaptists accepted with considerable zeal.

In responding to the challenge, two questions predominated: the implications of incorporating children into the covenant and the legal rights bestowed in baptism. The question of children and the covenant had been hotly debated in the early stages of the baptismal debate but had fallen from the field by 1646. Not, I believe, because the question was resolved, but because it was beyond resolution. For pedobaptists, it was a principal rationale for the baptism of infants. Those who refused baptism to infants similarly refused to admit the covenant argument as grounds for infant baptism. Now the anti-pedobaptists saw a way to use one of their opponents' principal arguments against them. If children could, in fact, be incorporated into the covenant, then they could receive the sacraments which were "the signs and seals of the covenant of grace."

A sense of the direction the arguments took can be seen from two quotations. In the first Daniel Featley makes a typical case for infant baptism on the covenant analogy; in the second Stephen Marshall demands that the consequences of admission to the covenant be taken seriously:

All they which receive the grace, both signified and exhibited to us in Baptisme, may and ought to receive the signs and Sacrament thereof. If God bestow upon children that which is greater, the inward grace; why should we denie them the lesser, the outward elements?...But children receive the grace signified and exhibition in baptisme: for the Apostle teacheth us, "they are not uncleane but holy": 1 Cor. 7:14 and therefore have both the remission of sins and sanctification. Ergo, children ought to receive the sign and sacrament thereof, to wit, baptisme.[15]

But if [children] being capable of the spiritual part, must intitle them to the outward signe, why then doe we not also admit them to the Sacrament of the Lords Supper, which is the seale of the Covenant of Grace, as well as the Sacrament of Baptisme? And this is urged, the rather because the Infants of the Jewes did eat of the Passover, as well as were circumcised, now if our Infants have every way as large a privilege as the Infants of the Jewes had, then we cannot deny them the same privilege which their Infants had, and consequently they must partake of the one Sacrament, as well as the other.[16]

The development of this argument, based on the parallel between the two covenants, caused the pedobaptists considerable embarrassment because they had relied so heavily on it as the cornerstone in their case for infant baptism.

Some attempted to distinguish between infants' right to the eucharist rather their right *in* it (*jus ad rem sed non jus in re*).[17] Others suggested that Jewish children did not eat the passover meal at all.[18] Neither argument proved convincing. Quite rightly, as Henry Denne remarked: "If you could bring such scripture for baptising Infants, as we are able to bring for Infants eating the Passover, the Controversie would soone be ended."[19]

But the controversy was not soon ended. Old arguments resurfaced and were once again put through the same mill and met the same refutation. There was, however, a notable shift among some of the pedobaptists. Perhaps the most remarkable was that of Jeremy Taylor. In his treatise *Of the Liberty of Prophesying*, Taylor engaged in a thorough examination of the baptismal controversy. In it he treated every point of conflict between the two sides and, in so doing, demonstrated a remarkable objectivity. He found weaknesses in the positions of both sides and suggested that the covenant motif alone is as weak a foundation for infant baptism as the insistence on articulate faith was for believers' baptism.

While Taylor's work did not bring the baptismal debate to an end, it did serve as a landmark. In all that followed, not one word was published calling into question either Taylor's arguments or his integrity in advancing them. Some openly admitted that nothing new could be added to the argument. Taylor's case came to be cited as authoritative by both pedobaptists and their opponents alike.

When, in the course of his study, Taylor turned to the communion of infants, he argued that infants ought either to have both sacraments or none at all. Coming from a pedobaptist such an opinion could not but bring a very different quality to the ongoing debate. In a most remarkable paragraph Taylor tried to change the character of the debate from polemic and invective to a search for the truth:

> Why shall men be more burthened with a prejudice
> and a name of obloquy, for not giving the Infants one
> Sacrament more than they are disliked for not affording them the other. If Anabaptist shall be a name of
> disgrace, why shall not some other name be invented

for them that deny to communicate Infants, which shall be equally disgraceful, or else both the opinions signified by such names, be accounted no disparagement, but receive their estimate according to their truth?[20]

Taylor returned to the question of communicating infants several times in the ensuing years. In *The Great Exemplar* he noted the practices of the primitive church and makes clear what is required of communicants and what is desirable but dependent on age and maturity:

> The primitive Church gave the Holy Sacrament to Infants immediately after Baptism, and by that act transmitted this proposition, that nothing was of absolute necessity but innocency and purity from sin, and a being in the state of grace; other actions of religion are excellent addition to the dignity of the person and honour of the mystery; but they were such of which Infants were not capable.[21]

In an age in which Christians were being excluded from the eucharist in great numbers, and for extended periods of time,[22] Taylor's remarks undercut both those who would exclude children from the sacrament as well as those who make knowledge the key to admission to the sacraments. In so doing, he clearly established that all those who may be baptized may also be communicated.

All this having been said, however, there is no contemporary evidence that anyone actually took measures to restore the communion of young children and infants. In an age of great theological controversy this is not surprising. When the very cause of pedobaptism itself was under such heavy attack, any new initiative could have shattered what little unity there was among those who continued to plead its cause. It was the same concern for unity which seemed to dissuade Taylor from strongly advocating the restoration of infant communion in *The Worthy Communicant.* Having demonstrated that the custom dates from the primitive church and remained the custom of the church for centuries, Taylor concluded that the communion of infants was lawful, but not necessary, and that for the peace of the church at that time, the question could be left at that.[23]

Put in the context of the time, Taylor's conclusion is understandable if not entirely commendable. The restoration of Charles II saw the Church of England make its last attempt to encompass the entirety of the religious spectrum and re-establish itself as the national church. (Even with this expressed intention, non-conforming ministers were being expelled from their cures by the hundreds.) Any attempt to make what would have been perceived as a radical shift in baptismal practice, even though the theological principles on which it was founded had been established in the context of bitter debate, would have been most unwise. The effect of any change in baptismal practice, at that time, could only have been to widen the gulf of theological opinion and make conformity even more difficult for those whose consciences were already hard pressed.

Thus, with the Restoration, the baptismal practice of the Church of England returned to a pattern not unlike that of the earlier part of the seventeenth century. The one exception was the introduction of the service of baptism for those "as are of riper years," there being many who had not been baptized as infants during the Commonwealth. The legacy of the baptismal debates was not, however, forgotten. The vast corpus of pamphlets in which the relationship between baptism and eucharist had been disputed was to affect generations to come.

## Infant Communion after the Restoration

It was only after the Church of England had begun to recover from the great damage inflicted during the Civil War and Commonwealth that some of the implications could be reflected upon anew. The pamphlets of the mid-century had a number of legatees.

James Peirce (c. 1674-1726), an English Presbyterian whom William Whiston called "the most learned of all the dissenting teachers I have known," was the first to write at length on the question. Working in a London congregation where the heritage of the tracts appears to have been very much alive, Peirce wrote the posthumously published *An Essay in Favour of the Ancient Practice of Giving the Eucharist to Children* (London, 1728). In the tract Peirce orders and rehearses all the arguments—biblical, historical, and pastoral—that had been advanced during the seventeenth century in favor of communicating baptized infants. In so doing he makes a very convincing case for the restoration of the practice not on the grounds of restoring a "primitivism" but rather on grounds of fidelity to a biblical understanding of initiation into the body of Christ and the relationship between baptism and eucharist. Peirce's understanding of the eucharist as the regular renewal of the baptismal covenant is quite remarkable for a time when the two sacraments were generally thought of as quite distinct realities. While Peirce's work was, in a sense, stillborn, in that it does not appear to have convinced local Presbyterians to start communicating young children, the work is a not unimportant monument to the debates of the previous century.

The other principal legatees of the debates were the Nonjurors. The usages controversy, which began in 1716 and is known primarily for the "four points,"[24] appears, from the beginning, also to have involved the question of infant communion. With the publication by Bishop Thomas Deacon of the *Compleat Collection of Devotions* (London, 1734), the prayer book of the Usagers, infant communion was the liturgical norm. Deacon's rationale for the practice is set out in his catechism-style *A full, true and comprehensive View of Christianity* (London, 1747).[25] Here it is obvious that Deacon had a good knowledge of the seventeenth-century debates, as well as being a beneficiary of the liturgical scholarship of Thomas Brett[26] and William Whiston[27] in addition to the devotional writings of John Kettlewell.[28] In twenty-three chapters of

"The Longer Catechism" Deacon expounds the scriptural warrant for the custom and its confirmation by tradition, answers "the objections which are usually made against it," and "represents the advantages of it." With the reconciliation of the Usagers and Non-Usagers around 1731 (on the Usagers' terms), infant communion remained normative in the practice of the Nonjurors until they were finally reabsorbed into the established church towards the end of the eighteenth century.

Other legatees of the baptismal controversies were the Wesleys. John Wesley was a communicant from the time he was eight years old. His father Samuel had grown up in a world imbued with the theological controversies of the mid-seventeenth century and was apparently prepared to act on some of them, at least as far as John was concerned. (From the relatively scarce data we have from the early eighteenth century, eight was a particularly early age to achieve communicant status.) The derivative effect on John was profound, as he, and the movement which bears his name, had no difficulty in admitting young children into the eucharistic fellowship, declaring: "That Infant communion was an abuse, I call upon you to prove."[29]

The final legatee of the seventeenth-century controversies was the Catholic Apostolic Church. This nineteenth-century movement stands as heir to both the baptismal debates and the Nonjurors. The published studies of its liturgical life[30] reveal it to be a remarkable combination of the charismatic and the catholic. No other tradition in the last two centuries could claim to have but one eucharist in each city on a Sunday, at which the local bishop presided, and at which all the baptized were communicants.

The tradition of infant communion does not return to what could technically be called Anglican circles until the end of the nineteenth century when Henry Holloway wrote *The Confirmation and Communion of Infants and Young Children* (London, 1901). Written at the instigation of Richard William Erraght, Vicar of Holy Trinity, Birmingham, who was imprisoned for ritualistic practices, the work has a lengthy preface by Lord Halifax. Halifax called the established age limits for confirmation and first communion "undoubtedly one of the worst abuses of the present time."[31] Holloway rehearses the historical evidence for infant "confirmation" and communion and then makes a lengthy case for the restoration of the practice, primarily on pastoral grounds. The effect of the work was to convince at least the "catholic-minded" bishops who read this sort of party literature to lower the established confirmation age, which had by this time risen to well into the teen years. These same bishops, however, were unwilling to administer the rite before candidates had reached the Tridentine age of seven. Since it was, of course, unthinkable to most Anglicans, since the advent of the strict churchmanship of the nineteenth century, to admit the uncon-firmed to communion, Holloway's work bore little fruit. The restoration of the communion of the very young had to wait at least another half-century.

## Modern Development

It is here that "hard data" become very difficult to obtain. A thumbnail sketch of what has transpired over this century must include several concurrent phenomena. The first is the Parish Communion movement. As a result of the popularization of the Parish Communion between the two World Wars, families began to attend the eucharist rather than Matins together each Sunday. This was a major shift in the pattern of Anglican church atten-dance. The other phenomenon was the Tractarian "children's mass" and its Broad Church equivalent, "children's church." The effect of these two contemporary movements on Anglicanism was to make children liturgical subjects once again. Their combined effect was to create a momentum in which it finally became neces-sary to "do something" with the children at the family eucharist.

As far as I am able to discern, sometime after the end of the Second World War, some parish clergy began to encourage patents to bring their children to the altar rail for a blessing at communion time rather than leaving them behind in the pews. Children, inquisitive as they are, began to ask, "Why can't I have some, too?" Some parents, incapable of giving a satisfactory answer, asked for help from the parish clergy. Some of the parochial clergy admitted they had no satisfactory answer either. The confirmation rubric ceased to make much sense when faced with younger children at the altar rail, some of whom were making, for their age, profound statements of faith (e.g., "I want Jesus").

By at the least the late 1950s there is evidence that some parochial clergy were communicating children as young as five years old. Once children this age had become communicants, it became very difficult to deny the sacrament to their younger siblings who also asked, "Why can't I have some, too?" It was not, however, until the various national doctrine committees had prepared their reports, and various liturgical commissions their new rites in the light of Resolution 25 of Lambeth 1968,[32] that there is any evidence for the restoration of the communion of all the baptized within Anglicanism. Since then the practice of communicating unconfirmed children, including the very young, has spread at a surprising rate (particularly considering the strict observance of the confirmation rubric, which since the nineteenth century had become a touchstone of modern Anglicanism). If a judgment can be made from recent collations of data for North America, it would appear that the practice is spreading widely and becoming deeply entrenched in the popular piety of considerable sections of our church.[33]

## Observations

Jeremy Taylor was right in his analysis of the question:
> Whether the Holy Communion may be given to Infants hath been a great question in the Church of God; which in this instance hath not been, as in others, divided by Parties and single Persons, *but by whole Ages...*[34]

For more than half its life (two-thirds at Taylor's time) the communion of all the baptized has been the normative practice of the universal church. The English Reformation took place during an age when the practice had virtually disappeared from most corners of Western Europe. But then so had the lay chalice and the custom of receiving communion more frequently than once a quarter. In an age in which any sense of eucharistic community had badly dissipated, the reformers' attempts to restore the weekly reception of communion and their successful restoration of the lay chalice should be seen as more surprising than their failure to restore the communion of young children and infants.

After four hundred years of the lay chalice and a century of the weekly eucharist (for the average North American Anglican, a couple of decades of the latter might approximate reality more closely), it is easy to forget what radical reforms these practices were when compared to the eucharistic faith and practice inherited by our forebears. That the Anglican Communion as a whole should be moving towards the restoration of the communion of all the baptized should be no more surprising than any of the other eucharistic reforms that have taken place within our tradition during its lifetime.

During an age in which the eucharist was celebrated rarely, and on the occasions it was celebrated there being relatively few communicants, it is hardly surprising that the question of infant communion was raised as a question of theory rather than one of practice. It should be no less surprising that the question is pressed as a practical one when the Sunday eucharist, at which all the baptized are present, has become the normative practice. It is here that our overview of history is helpful. Whenever the church has come to see itself as a small, gathered, eucharistic community, the communion of all the baptized quickly becomes a real question. This can be seen in the eucharistic practice of both the Nonjurors and the Catholic Apostolic Church. Similarly, when the church sees itself as established, encompassing the whole of society, there is little question of communicating all the baptized. In the former it is the regular reception of the eucharist that sustains and nurtures the Christian community; in the latter it is social structure, rather than the sacraments, that maintains the fabric of the church. It is clear in which of these ages we live.

Taylor was also right when he suggested:

> And after all, the refusing to Communicate Infants entered into the Church upon an unwarrantable ground; for though it was confessed that the Communion would do them benefit, yet it was denied to them when the doctrine of transubstantion entered....[35]

The withdrawal of communion from the very young is as lamentable as the withdrawal of the chalice from the laity. They were done, in fact, for the same reason: an exaggerated sense of the possible abuse of the second species.[36] The reformers succeeded in righting part of that abuse of eucharistic practice. The seventeenth-century debate established that the other part of the abuse, the exclusion of children from the table, was also susceptible of redress. The authenticity of the historical practice had been admitted since the early days of the Reformation. The theological legitimacy of the practice had been conceded first in the midst of heated combat and again, later, in the clearer light of a re-established Church of England.

As an Anglican it seems to me very difficult to reject a practice when it is acknowledged as an historic practice of the universal church and when the theological tradition acknowledges that the practice is founded on the self-same principles that legitimate infant baptism. When those two realities are placed in the context of contemporary Anglican eucharistic practice—the weekly communion at which the whole community is present—it is very difficult to see why we would even consider not admitting all the baptized to the eucharist. To do so is to disregard both history and what is admitted as theological truth. To do either is very un-Anglican indeed.

# Notes

1. Lambeth Conference 1968, *Resolutions and Reports* (London: SPCK, 1968), pp. 37, 99.

2. This line of argumentation is followed in papers written by two bishops opposed to the restoration of the communion of all the baptized: Reginald Hollis, "Reflections on the Statement on Christian Initiation" (presented to the Canadian General Synod at Calgary, August 1977) and C. FitzSimons Allison, "A Working Paper on Initiatory Rites" (prepared for the House of Bishops Meeting, San Antonio, 1986), now published as "Anglican Initiatory Rites: A Contribution to the Current Debate," *Anglican and Episcopal History* 56 (1987): 27-43.

3. Peter J. Jagger, *Clouded Witness: Initiation in the Church of England in the Mid-Victorian Period, 1850-1875* (Allison Park, Penn: Pickwick, 1982), presents an important study of the evolution of our present-day initiation practices.

4. Thomas Cartwright, *A Replye to an answere made of M. Doctor Whitegifte againste the Admonition to the Parliament* (London, 1573), pp. 143f.

5. Thomas Morton, *A Catholicke Appeal for Protestants, Out of the Confessions of the Romane Doctors* (London, 1610), pp. 136-38, 244f; and *Of the Institution of the Sacrament of the Blessed Bodie and Blood of Christ, (by some called) the Masse of Christ* (London, 1631), pp. 38-40.

6. William Ames, *A Fresh Suit Against Human Ceremonies in Gods Worship* (London, 1633), pt. 2, p. 37.

7. This stands in marked contrast to the reform of initiation practices which took place a century and a half earlier in the Bohemian Reformation; cf. David R. Holeton, "The Communion of Infants and Hussitism," *Communio Viatorum* 27 (1984): 207-25; "The Communion of Infants: The Basel Years," *Communio Viatorum* 29 (1986): 15-40; and *La Communion des tout-petits enfants: Etude du mouvement*

*eucharistique en Bohême à la fin du Moyen-Age* (Rome: Edizioni Liturgiche, 1987).

8. Edward Barber, *A Small Treatise of Baptisme, or, Dipping* (London, 1641), p. 18.

9. The medieval period produced a number of paradigms to interpret the sacraments, including legal and medicinal models. The survival of the biological model in post-Reformation England reflects both the tenacity of this particular paradigm and its adaptability to a two-sacrament theology that made other models untenable.

10. John Tombes, *Anti-paedobaptism; or the second part of the full review of the Dispute concerning Infant-Baptism* (London, 1654), p. 37.

11. Thomas Fuller, *The Infants Advocate* (London, 1653), p. 107.

12. Richard Baxter, *Certain Disputations of Right to Sacraments, and the true nature of visible Christianity* (London, 1657), p. 120.

13. Henry Haggar, *The Foundation of the Font Discovered* (London, 1653), pp. 66f.

14. Richard Baxter, *Certain Disputations*, p. 114.

15. Daniel Featley, Καταβαπτισται καταπτυστοι. *The Dippers dipt. or, The Anabaptists Duck'd and Plunged over Head and Eares, at a Disputation in Southwark* (London, 1645), pp. 48f.

16. Stephen Marshall, *A Sermon of the Baptizing of Infants* (London, 1644), p. 51.

17. Here they follow Thomas Aquinas, *Summa Theologica* III, q. 73, a. 3.

18. In so doing their argument is often drawn from Ioh. Maldonatus, *Commentarii in Quatuor Evangelistas* (Mussiponti, 1596), in Ioh 6:54, col. 713ff, where Maldonatus rehearses the arguments used against the Bohemians who interpreted the text in a sacramental, rather

than spiritual, sense. Cf. Samuel Chidley, *A Christian Plea for Infants Baptisme* (London, 1644), pp. 85-87.

19. Henry Denne, *Antichrist Unmasked in Two Treaties* (London, 1645), p. 29.

20. Jeremy Taylor, *Of the Liberty of Prophesying* (London, 1648), XVIII, 18 (ed. Heber 8:159f).

21. Jeremy Taylor, *The Great Exemplar* (London, 1655), XIX, 15 (ed. Heber 3:309). In the same work Taylor remarks, "Certainly there is infinitely more reason why infants may be communicated, than why they may not be baptized" (I, 8, vi [ed. Heber 2:295]).

22. Thomas Hickes, *A Letter or Word of Advice to the Saints, Known and Unknown* (London, 1653), p. 4, complains that "there are many thousands about the city of London that have not received [communion] for seven or eight years" and that "young men and maids" are coming to the age of twenty-five and still have never received communion (ibid., p. 6). Giles Firmin, *A Sober Reply to the Sober Answer of Reverend Mr. Cawdrey* (London, 1655), Foreword, remarks: "I saw Presbyteriall Brethern keep back half or three quarters of their Churches from the Lords Supper, and that for divers years together, yet did so constantly baptise their children, I thought with myselfe, where have these men a ground for this practice?"

23. Jeremy Taylor, *The Worthy Communicant* (London, 1661), III, 2 (ed. Heber 15:501ff).

24. (1) Prayers for the faithful departed, (2) the Mixed Chalice, (3) the Epiclesis on the elements in the eucharistic prayer, and (4) the recitation of the Prayer of Oblation immediately after the Prayer of Consecration.

25. Pp. 343-93.

26. *A Collection of the Principal Liturgies Used by the Christian Church in the Celebration of the Holy Eucharist* (London,

1720) was the first fruit readily available in English of the new liturgiological passion for collecting primitive liturgies.

27. *Primitive Christianity Reviv'd*, vol. II: *The Constitutions of the Apostles by Clement* (London, 1711). The widespread acceptance of this text as a witness to apostolic practice gave it the same authority in determining the authenticity of a practice as the work of Ps.-Dionysius the Areopagite had enjoyed until the fifteenth century. Whiston's translation made an "apostolic authority" for the communion of infants available to those, like the Nonjurors, who valued the primitive church as primary model for contemporary practice.

28. *An Help and Exhortation to Worthy Communicating* (London, 1683). In this often reprinted devotional manual Kettlewell tries to strike a balance between 1 Cor 11.28 and John 6.53. He argues that, while we cannot come to the eucharist unworthily, neither can we hold back: "For [the eucharist] is no more, than is expressly spoke of in *Baptism*, which is but *of equal rank with it*, both *being Duties, and equally required.* For of that 'tis said, *He that believes, and is baptized, shall be saved* Mark 16:16. And except a Man be born. Thus necessary is it for all Men" (8th edition, 1717, pp. 89f).

29. Henry Holloway, *The Confirmation and Communion of Infants and Young Children* (London: Skeffington, 1901), p. iii.

30. Cf. Kenneth Stevenson, "The Catholic Apostolic Church—Its History and Its Eucharist," *Studia Liturgica* 13 (1979): 21-45.

31. Holloway, *The Confirmation*, p. xxiii.

32. A summary of these can be found in David R. Holeton, "Christian Initiation in Some Anglican Provinces," *Studia Liturgica* 12 (1977): 129-50.

33. A survey conducted by Gwen Bright and Esther North of Canadian practice in 1985 showed that the communion of all the baptized is widespread in urban dioceses. Research by Richard Hatfield for an S.T.M. thesis at Nashotah House also

showed the practice deeply entrenched in various parts of the Episcopal Church (U.S.A.).

34. Jeremy Taylor, *The Worthy Communicant* (London, 1661), III, 2 (ed. Heber 15:501f).

35. Ibid. (ed. Heber 15:507).

36. The practice has a number of medieval witnesses including Ps.-Hugh of St. Victor (Robertus Paululus), *De officiis ecclesiasticis* I, 12 (*PL* 177: 388) and Thomas of Chobham, *Summa confessorum* a. 4 d. 2 q. 4 (ed. F. Broomfield [Louvain and Paris: Nauwelaerts, 1968], pp. 105f).

# 4

# A Theological Reflection on the Experience of Inclusion/Exclusion at the Eucharist

*Kenneth W. Stevenson*

There are many ways in which one may distinguish between when a person is "included" in the eucharist and when "excluded." For example, when I go to a celebration of the eucharist in a Greek Orthodox cathedral, I participate in a way comparable to many of the other worshipers (given that I arrive with the considerable handicap of being a liturgist), simply because only a small minority actually receive the eucharistic bread and wine. On the other hand, when I attend (as I once did) a eucharist according to the Byzantine rite in a small Melkite church, I am ushered up to take my place in line with the other communicants, as a genuine ecumenical gesture from the Roman Catholic Church to a visiting Anglican. All this is to say the obvious: the revival of eucharistic faith and practice in the twentieth century places us in a context, and the context is that, when we consider the admission of children to communion, we are indeed doing so at a particular time when they *feel excluded* in a way which would not have been true, say, in seventeenth-century baroque Catholicism or eighteenth-century Evangelicalism.

I have been asked to offer a "theological reflection," but I would like to stress at the outset that what follows is really a "theological reflection upon another theological reflection," and that primary reflection was going on inside me as a child.

## Three Christian Traditions

What I am about to describe is part travelography, part family history, part liturgical variety. It is about the experience of the interaction of three Christian traditions in the eucharistic life of a growing child. Because I was that child, I shall do my best not to be sentimental, not to lay it on too thick. There is no element of tragedy in it, because I enjoyed those three traditions and did not regret their separation. And I suppose it partly stems from the fact that I have a vivid mind, a wild imagination, an eye for beautiful things, an ear for good music. Not to put too fine a point on it, I have always enjoyed going to church. Moreover, as I try to put together my thoughts in some sort of not too jumbled order, I cast my mind back to 1979, the International Year of the Child, when many of us were reminded, sometimes somewhat forcibly, that children are *not* small adults, but are people in their own right. Such, I think, is the basis on which the patristic church could dare to give communion to young persons.

I was born in 1949. My parents met just after the Second World War, in Denmark. My father, himself half-Danish, had been drafted into MI6 in 1940 because he spoke Danish (his mother had brought him up virtually bilingual). But my father's family had roots in the Catholic Apostolic Church. His father had been an "angel" (or bishop) in the congregation in Edinburgh, and his mother's family was involved in many ways in that church in Denmark. Then along comes my mother, a "war-bride," the daughter of the Lutheran bishop of Århus, just to add another flavor to this rich religious cocktail.

While the Catholic Apostolic Church was at its strongest in Denmark and in Lutheran parts of Germany, it was relatively weak in the British Isles, even though it started its life in England in the 1830s.[1] By an early stage, probably while its liturgy was becoming increasingly enriched, children were admitted to communion on the following terms. First communion came soon after baptism, when the celebrant gave the baby the species with the aid of a spoon. Thereafter, children received communion on special occasions (the main festivals of Christmas, Easter, Pentecost, and All Saints) from an early age, depending on circumstances. Children were received into regular communion by the local angel (bishop) at the age of eleven, after which they could receive communion at any service.[2] The final stage in Catholic Apostolic initiation was "sealing," with the laying on of hands by the Apostle, a rite which included anointing with chrism. This took place at the age of eighteen, after a course of instruction. The last Apostle died in 1901, terminating ordinations, and signalling the eventual demise of the church. "Sealing" made no difference to receiving communion, but I mention it in passing as yet one more variant in the way the Western churches have responded to historical inquiry and new patterns of religious experience and sacramental life.[3]

From the late 1840s and 1850s, such a scheme operated in Catholic Apostolic congregations, so that by the 1950s it was unquestioned—*de rigeur* in fact—that babies and small children should receive communion wherever manpower allowed the eucharist to be celebrated. In fact, I was lucky because the Edinburgh church had a priest right through to Easter 1958, when he died at the age of 89. Because of his advanced age and the length of the liturgy, he only celebrated the eucharist (latterly) once a month, then only at festivals. I cannot recall a eucharist in that church when I did *not* receive communion. I can also remember one occasion when we attended the eucharist in the little church in Århus on a family Christmas holiday in 1954; there must have been others as well.

"Ambience" has a great effect on a child, and I was no exception. The Edinburgh church was a large Victorian building, designed by Rowand Anderson. It was neo-romanesque in style, with open space to make visibility as good as possible. The acoustics were terrible, but since the liturgy was usually intoned, that didn't matter. We would walk in through the vestibule, get our books from one of the doorkeepers or underdeacons, and we would go halfway up the left-hand side and occupy a (relatively) comfortable pew.

I don't remember all the details of the liturgy itself, but certain things stick in my mind, built up from this intermittent experience of the church. The entry of the ministers made quite an impression; it would consist of a small group of acolytes, and they would be followed by a group of elderly underdeacons, and at the end, in increasing old age, one could hear the shuffling feet of the celebrant. (I do vaguely remember a deacon.) All these ministers wore what we would call cassock and surplice, except the celebrant, who wore an alb, stole, and chasuble (the latter two invariably white, and cut in the gothic style).

Other parts that stick in my mind are the presentation of the tithes and offerings, because that involved more movement, this time from the rear of the church (the introit was from the side), and the Great Entrance, when the vessels were moved from the Table of Prothesis (in the upper choir) to the altar. But the climax always came when the family received communion together. Playing it by the book, the Edinburgh congregation restricted administration to the priest and the deacon.[4] When the old deacon died, it meant that only the priest administered to a congregation of about a hundred. Underdeacons hovered, replenishing the chalice from a large flagon (I remember once when this happened just before I communicated) and keeping an eye on the priest who right at the end of his life gave communion seated, so that we came up in pairs. Once (so I was told by someone in the congregation whom we knew well), I responded to the eucharistic gifts with the expression "Ta" instead of the customary "Amen," but I don't remember any rebuff! Children were not given communion with any special motives or conditions. It was expected, natural, right. The liturgy, with its strong ecclesiology, and no doubt strengthened by the heightened atmosphere of a church getting ready to disappear, was enough of a binding force to what went on. I think what I remember most was the way my parents just let us experience this liturgy, with a bit of explanation here and there.

I have dwelt on this at some length, because it is the most unfamiliar of the three traditions. But let me now come to the second.

Catholic Apostolics were usually told to become Anglicans. That held good of soldiers going to the front in the two World Wars, and also of those families that belonged to the church towards the end of its life. This meant that my intermittent experience of a long, late morning liturgy, in the Edinburgh Catholic Apostolic Church, was supplemented by a weekly attendance at the local Episcopal church at 8:00 in the morning. (In those days, Matins was the normal service at 11:00 in the country churches.) The Episcopal Church in Scotland has a peculiar ambience. It is made up of two strands, the old Scottish "strict" tradition, which still has in its corporate memory Jacobite loyalties and persecution under the Hanoverians, together with its high theology of the eucharist from the seventeenth- and eighteenth-century divines. The other strand is the English "liberal" tradition, breathing the atmosphere of the English abroad, using the 1662 liturgy (*not* the Scottish 1929).[5] I was lucky in experiencing both these strands in two different congregations for the 8:00 eucharist. I was certainly not aware of all these hidden skeletons, but they were definitely in the background.

At this 8:00 eucharist, attended by only a small number, I soon realized both the *differences* from and the *similarities* to the Catholic Apostolic service. The priest was considerably younger. The service was part of a regular diet which the congregation could (in the best sense) "take for granted." I remember the colors of the vestments changing and that the service was always *said*. The genuflection of the celebrant (and one or two of the congregation) during the Nicene Creed was another thing that was noticeable to the wandering eye. But one thing I could not fail to notice: I never, *ever* went up to the altar rail because I was not allowed to receive communion.

I didn't question this rule—one didn't in those days. In retrospect, it now seems clear that the reason my parents had me confirmed at Christmas 1958 was that my brother and I had been deprived of the eucharist altogether since the death, that Easter, of the last Catholic Apostolic priest. I remember the friendliness of the Episcopal clergy to me, since I seemed to take an interest in religious things. After confirmation, I became an acolyte, then a choir-boy, and so on up the ranks. I was soon caught up in many of the activities of a local congregation. But I looked back, and still do, to my earlier experiences, and informed myself better on the how and why, which became quite a mystagogical experience, perhaps even therapeutic. That all became a Ph.D. thesis in 1975.[6]

The third tradition stemmed from the family holidays. Each summer we would spend a month in Denmark with my mother's relations. My grandfather was interested in much of what we did, and, insofar as one can take seriously the decision of a boy of four years to be ordained, he was proud of the fact that *one* of his offspring wanted to follow what for him was the family trade (he was the sixth consecutive Lutheran pastor in his family). Every Sunday we would attend a Lutheran church, whether the cathedral in Århus or a local village church. But we would also go to special occasions, such as the diocesan synod service, which usually coincided with the holiday in early August, and ordinations. My grandfather really had to act as a double, because my father's father had died long before I was born. He was a towering, noisy, flamboyant Dane, with an active interest in English philosophical theology (my parents frowned on that interest!), entomology, and his vast rural diocese, which he seemed to know like the back of his hand.

I emphasize these family claims because they provided my *entrée* into this very *national* of Western churches. The buildings remain vivid in my mind, because they were so different: whitewashed inside, usually with a lot of medieval art surviving, an organ in the west gallery, pastor in cassock and ruff, and alb and chasuble atop when at the altar. The liturgical movement was just stirring in Denmark through the 1950s, building up to what it is now, with ever-increasing numbers of communicants.[7] Wherever possible, my parents took us to communion. I remember occasions when we children remained in our seats. I also remember occasions when we went to the altar-rail, enjoying the Lutheran practice there of holding out a small silver cup, while the celebrant poured the wine from a large chalice equipped with a spout. Again, similarities and differences occurred to me, other than the language. I remember enjoying the solemnity of Lutheran worship, and the organ interludes always added something of a bonus, especially in Århus cathedral (whose organ was restored along neo-baroque lines in 1927 partly through my grandfather's friendship with Albert Schweitzer). The visual aspects of worship made considerable impact. Word and sacrament belonged together, but they had different symbolisms, as the pastor wore vestments at the altar, but stripped down to cassock and ruff for the sermon and intercessions at the pulpit. Although we often left the church for the sermon (for understandable reasons), I remember the feeling of expectation by the congregation when the sermon began. A good Danish Lutheran congregation expects a decent sermon. That was *not* something I had experienced before. The Catholic Apostolic priest was too aged (although in its halcyon days that church would have had a homily at every Sunday morning eucharist) and the Episcopalians never preached at the early service, though they did at Matins, but I regarded that strange post-monastic office as something to endure rather than enjoy, so it didn't begin to compete with Danish delights. I referred to the "solemnity" of the Lutheran service; this was heightened at the communion, where each row of communicants was dismissed by a prayer, and the choir would halt during their communion hymn while the organ would improvise. Unlike the Anglican mini-sermon ("Take and eat this in remembrance that Christ died for thee, and feed on him in thy heart by faith, with thanksgiving" and "Drink this in remembrance that Christ's blood was shed for thee, and be thankful"), the Danish celebrant would declare the fact of redemption in this short prayer, which ended with the peace and the sign of the cross made with the chalice. Once more, the symbolism and the context made a great impression on me. It was part of the holiday.

The three traditions, then, were a varied eucharistic diet on which I fed at various stages for family reasons. Each had its own context, and there was never any sense of clash. The Catholic Apostolic eucharist was what I experienced on special occasions. I was welcome at its altar. The Episcopal eucharist was the regular Sunday 8:00 celebration. I was only welcome there after confirmation, which, in a largely Presbyterian country, was felt very strongly as a social and religious boundary. Then, every summer, the Danish Lutheran Church impinged on my religious experience in a big way. Sometimes we took communion, sometimes not; after confirmation, we always did. As I grew up, I began to realize how strongly my parents felt that we should receive communion. The Catholic Apostolics, with their single corporate Sunday eucharist at which everyone took communion (including—if they wished—visitors from other churches), had got it right, whereas the Anglicans had got it wrong. I remember, too, at a later age, learning that the first Lutheran Bishop of Sjaelland, Peder Palladius, wanted children to receive communion from the age of six or seven.[8] His high Lutheranism didn't survive later Lutheran so-called "orthodoxy," but there is now pressure for children to receive before Lutheran confirmation, and any antecedents, however anomalous, are grist to the mill of those championing the cause. Professor Christian Thodberg of Århus University tells me that the controversy began as far back as 1880.[9] In view of the fact that Catholic Apostolic congregations existed in many parts of Denmark, I should not be at all surprised if there were not some indirect feedback from the new church to the old folk-church. History is full of ironies.

## A Synthesis

As I try to put these three strands together, I must begin by saying, without any qualification whatever, that I never felt that any one of the three churches was considered "wrong" by us, except on the question of admission to communion. I regarded, as did my parents, the three churches as three different, overlapping experiences. They helped me to enjoy the matter of *choice* and *option*. It was later on that I was to discover the fullness of the riches of the Catholic Apostolic heritage. I think that this is an important point to make, particularly when we consider today the question of children from what the latest jargon calls, in its inevitably clinical manner, an "inter-church marriage." Children are not fools. They don't necessarily think that if something happens in one way in one place, it's wrong if it doesn't happen in another. We live in a world full of choices and options. It should come as no surprise that the Christian churches should express these things as well.

Second, I did feel committed to all three of those churches, and still do, because I arrived on three different kinds of church doorsteps as a direct result of family commitment. In later years this helped me to range further afield, and as a student who was also an ordinand, I often surprised local clergy by spending a lot of time being a spiritual nomad, moving from church to church, to see what it was like. The conviction that spiritual nomadry is right for many students was strengthened after I became a university chaplain. I remember hearing of Archbishop Michael Ramsey's reaction to a particularly complex report on theological education: "The best thing you can do with ordinands is to leave them alone." But I still harbored in my underlying attitudes the feeling that there were some churches where I was a welcome communicant, some where I was tolerated, others where I should stay in my place, though this latter category diminished somewhat after Vatican II, as I became a regular communicant at Roman Catholic altars when on holiday in France, Belgium, and Germany. Communion *does* involve commitment, but some of the mistakes of the eucharistic revival in the Western churches have been that it has sharpened the boundaries between "regular" and "occasional," to such a degree that the "occasional" feels cut off, whether the "occasional" is a visitor from another church (even another country) or is someone who only comes to church at Christmas.

Third, we adults continue to underestimate the importance for children of the visual and the significant role played by context, rather than text, in the celebration of the liturgy. The Catholic Apostolic experience was a drama in itself. We entered through the west door; we sat in our pews; we went up to the altar; then, after the service, we were allowed to walk round the building and become used to it, meeting people, seeing carvings, passages, light-switches, vestments. For me, all this was of vital importance, and I suppose it built up within me a healthy suspicion of that type of Western Protestantism and Tridentine Catholicism that seeks to impose on the liturgy what people are *supposed* to believe—what Aidan Kavanagh has referred to as "secondary theology."[10] I once talked to an upright and pious student who was thinking about being ordained. Part of his problem was that he was trying to think, all the time, about what God was teaching him, at any given moment. "The trouble with some of you Evangelicals," I replied, "is that you are so determined that God is *teaching* you, when in fact God might be loving you, affirming you, even enjoy-ing you."

Fourth, as we embark nowadays on admitting children to com-munion, I think there is a grave danger in trying to predetermine what they will experience. It was obviously a joy for my parents to take me to a church where I would be a welcome and natural com-municant. But the catechesis I received was the liturgy itself, with snatches here and there of explanation and back-up.[11] Later on, as a teenager, I rebelled and argued and quarrelled and sifted through the family corporate memory and identified myself and those parts of my own contemporary Christianity which fed me. We all have to move on. But predetermination is not something you will find in the baptismal pro-catechesis of the fourth-century fathers. I remember Father Ted Yarnold once addressing a gathering in London on his beloved fourth-century homilists and ending the answer to a penetrating question with the throw-away, "Someone really ought to analyze these baptismal catechists from the point of view of modern educational psychology."[12] My experience was my experience was my experience, and it *was* different when I could take communion. I knew it was important, for the liturgy led up to it, deliberately, with its rhythms and changes. I am not arguing for obscurantism. But I am pleading for a basic *trust* in the liturgy to do its own job.

Fifth, the experience of exclusion is a painful one, whether or not the exclusion is questioned, whether or not it is explained.[13] But the exclusion was not just me, at the Episcopalian services, before I was confirmed. It divides families. The eucharist, we keep telling ourselves, is a corporate activity of the whole church. When families are divided within themselves, whether because one or two children are not confirmed, or because in other instances husband or wife belongs to another church, exclusion is a form of spiritual blackmail. I do not wish to seem to argue the case for admitting children to communion. This is another's task.[14] But the case rears its head when the child in question knows both inclusion and exclusion. To put it bluntly, I identified with the Catholic Apostolic eucharist, for all its length and my impatience with a protracted communion due to the age of the priest that forced him to administer the elements sitting in his chair. The sacred was allowed me there, in that strange, nineteenth-century church which has so much else to teach Christianity, whereas the sacred was *not* given me, down the road, at the local Episcopalian tabernacle.

Sixth, for a child word and symbol go closely together. That is something which many modern educational approaches are building upon, and rightly so. That makes me ask myself, in retrospect, why it was that I could "hear" the word preached Episcopalian-style (for all that it was usually done at Matins), and yet I was not able to "hear" the sacrament by partaking of the bread and wine. Perhaps multiple printing and trivializing of preaching have made us lose out on the real purpose of the ministry of the word to such a degree that all we have left is the eucharist.[15] As we rediscover the interaction of words and symbolism, of children and older people, of community and individual, in ways that are appropriate for *our* century, so we may also rediscover the inevitable interaction and inseparable nature of word and sacrament at the Table of the Lord.

Seventh, and finally, for me, living with three churches at a time, age meant very little. Confirmation at the age of nine was a means of receiving communion. The Spirit had already been given at baptism, as my own baptismal liturgy taught me. The Spirit was also being given and experienced in a whole series of intermeshing activities and reflections on life and faith. I have grave doubts about the popularity today of the age limit of six or seven. It's arbitrary, adultist, and in no sense an important age *for the child* as the child experiences it. Let me end with one more anecdote, to illustrate. The last diocese in which I was a presbyter has recently embarked on a controlled experiment, which allows for congregations, with the agreement of the parents, to admit children to communion from the age of seven; confirmation would then, it is half-expected, be delayed until the mid/late teens.[16] Before this was formally passed by our Diocesan Synod, two local Ecumenical Projects in the diocese went ahead with their own experiments, one of which was the Higher Education Chaplaincy, where I was to work and serve. I therefore arrived on the scene after my congregation had agreed to move forward, but before the diocese had debated and agreed on the issue. We were as a family happy with this innovation. In due course, both my daughters became regular communicants. But what of my son? Technically, the answer was "no" until he reached the magic age. He, therefore, was excluded. And, of course, when I was a visiting preacher in other parishes which have *not* taken up the new option, technically my daughters should not be communicants either. However, in 1984 my family holidayed in Denmark and stayed with various relations and friends. On the Sunday, we all went to the morning eucharist at Århus cathedral, a building full of family memories, and where my grandfather is still remembered. James was five that summer. He announced, "I want communion." He remembered being in Århus two years earlier, so it was for him a special occasion, returning to the familiar. For all sorts of reasons, I decided to throw my Anglican loyalties to the winds, and I made a gut-reaction, back to my own experience as a child; and up he came. Just to add a piquant note, the long communion hymn was one of Nikolai Grundtvig's compositions, "Rejs op dit hoved, al kristenhed"[17] ("Lift up your heads, all Christianity"), a hymn that rejoices in the nearness of the Kingdom, the fullness of Christian hope. It all seemed the most natural thing in the world.

## Notes

1. See K. W. Stevenson, "The Catholic Apostolic Church—Its History and Its Eucharist," *Studia Liturgica* 13 (1979): 21-45.

2. See *Book of Regulations* (London: Strangeways, 1878), 15ff. The recommendation is that children should be "phased" into regular communion, starting with the main festivals, then monthly, then the blessing and reception into regular communion. Local ministers and parents played a significant role in the formal and informal catechesis.

3. See Paul J. Roberts, "The Pattern of Initiation: Sacrament and Experience in the Catholic Apostolic Church and Its Implications for Modern Liturgical and Theological Debate," Ph.D. dissertation, Manchester University, 1990.

4. Other congregations employed underdeacons for the administration of the chalice in later years.

5. For these two strands, see Marion Lochhead, *Episcopalian Scotland in the Nineteenth Century* (London: Murray, 1966).

6. K. W. Stevenson, "The Catholic Apostolic Eucharist," Ph.D. dissertation, Southampton University, 1975. See section on this liturgy in *Coena Domini* II.

7. Much of the liturgical movement in Denmark has been marked by recovery of classical Lutheran features in worship,

rather than by the adoption of new liturgical texts; hymnody and music have played an important role. See Christian Thodberg, "Grundtvig the Hymnwriter," in *N.F.S. Grundtvig: Tradition and Renewal*, ed. Chr. Thodberg and A. Thyssen (Copenhagen: Den Danske Selskab, 1983), pp. 160ff.

8. See H. Haar, ed., *Peder Palladius; En Visitatsbog* (Copenhagen: Haase, 1940), p. 68, where Palladius uses Mark 10.14 in support of children coming early to communion. The Visitation Book dates from September 1541; see p. 52, where Palladius stresses the need for parents to take young children to church, and for them to walk up and down the aisles to keep them quite; the editor notes the demise of Palladius' recommendations about early communion (p. 168, n. 11).

9. Conversation with Christian Thodberg, Århus, during August 1984.

10. Aidan Kavanagh, *On Liturgical Theology* (New York: Pueblo Publishing Co., 1984).

11. See *Book of Regulations* 16 (sections 535f).

12. See E. J. Yarnold, "Initiation: Sacrament and Experience," in *Liturgy Reshaped*, ed. Kenneth Stevenson (London: SPCK, 1982), pp. 17-31.

13. See D. R. Holeton, "The Communion of Infants and Younger Children," in *...and do not hinder them*, ed. G. Müller-Fahrenholz, Faith and Order Paper 109 (Geneva: World Council of Churches, 1982), p. 68, where Holeton recounts my experience from which this paper developed.

14. See D. R. Holeton, *Infant Communion—Then and Now*, Grove Liturgical Study 27 (Bramcote, Nott.: Grove Books, 1981).

15. See, for example, Kavanagh, *On Liturgical Theology*, pp. 103ff, for a discussion of the not always beneficial effect of the invention of printing on worship.

16. A Pastoral Letter from the Diocesan Bishop to All Clergy,

Diocese of Manchester, May 1983. This followed a debate at Diocesan Synod, December 1982, at which a report was discussed, prepared by a committee under the chair of the Right Rev. Prof. R. P. C. Hanson.

17. *Den Danske Salmebog* (Copenhagen: Haase, 1985), n. 229.

## 5

# American Perspectives: (i) The Place of Baptismal Anointing

*Leonel L. Mitchell*

### Consignation

In the 1979 American revision of the Book of Common Prayer, the consignation with chrism was restored to the baptismal rite. The exact form this act takes is that, following the baptismal washing in the name of the Trinity, the bishop or, in the bishop's absence, the priest who is presiding, "at a place in full sight of the congregation," prays over the neophytes, saying,

> Heavenly Father, we thank you that by water and the Holy Spirit you have bestowed upon *these* your *servants* the forgiveness of sin, and have raised *them* to the new life of grace. Sustain *them*, O Lord, in your Holy Spirit. Give *them* an inquiring and discerning heart, the courage to will and to persevere, a spirit to know and to love you, and the gift of joy and wonder in all your works. (BCP 1979, p. 308)

The prayer is a retranslation into contemporary English of the prayer *ad consignandum* from the Gelasian and Gregorian Sacramentaries, a prayer which is the central prayer of confirmation in the prayer book of 1662,[1] but was anciently a part of the baptismal rite.

Following the prayer, the rite proceeds:

> *Then the Bishop or Priest places a hand on the person's*

*head, marking on the forehead the sign of the cross*
*[using Chrism if desired] and saying to each one*

N., you are sealed by the Holy Spirit in Baptism and
marked as Christ's own forever. *Amen.*

The models for this consignation are the Mozarabic and
Gallican usages, which include a single post-baptismal chrismation
as a part of the consignation of the forehead.[2] It is, in fact, possible
that the Mozarabic liturgy, which was clearly known to Cranmer
and from which he drew the blessing of the font in 1549,[3] was also
Cranmer's inspiration for the chrismation in 1549 and for the
consignation with which he replaced it in 1552. This post-baptismal consignation has been a consistent element of Anglican baptismal practice since that time, in spite of Puritan protests.[4]

Marion Hatchett has written extensively concerning the meaning of this consignation, and the formula which Cranmer associated with it:

> We...do sign *him* with the sign of the Cross, in token
> that hereafter *he* shall not be ashamed to confess the
> faith of Christ crucified, and manfully to fight under
> his banner, against sin, the world, and the devil; and
> to continue Christ's faithful soldier and servant unto
> *his* life's end.[5]

He describes it as a succinct summary of the meaning of the
"peculiar second anointing of the Roman rite which was called
'confirmation'"[6] and suggests that Cranmer intended this ceremony to be identified with the medieval *consignatio frontis*, which was
generally called confirmation.

## The Theological Significance of the Signing

To say all this, however, is not to imply that there is any theological consensus, even within the American Episcopal Church, concerning the meaning of the post-baptismal consignation. A variety
of opinions are in fact held.

One view is that the consignation is an explanatory ceremony, like the giving of a baptismal candle, which serves to make explicit some of the meaning intrinsic to baptism itself. Its use is seen as in no way essential to the rite. The seal of the Holy Spirit to which the formula refers is conferred in baptism itself. The seal is, in fact, the inward and spiritual grace of baptism. In general terms this is the view ably put forward by G. W. H. Lampe in *The Seal of the Spirit.*[7]

At the opposite end of the spectrum is the view that the consignation is that rite which Catholics have generally called confirmation and is a distinct sacramental act necessary for the completion of Christian initiation. The position can, of course, be identified with that of Gregory Dix in *The Theology of Confirmation in Relation to Baptism.*[8] Many of those who hold this view would see the use of episcopally consecrated chrism as necessary for the consignation, while others would see the signing with the cross itself as the necessary act, and the use of the chrism to be a desirable, meaningful, but not strictly necessary addition to the rite.

A third position is that originally expounded by Rabanus Maurus, the ninth-century archbishop of Mainz, who described the post-baptismal chrismation this way:

> For after the baptized has ascended from the font,
> immediately he is signed on the head by a presbyter
> with holy chrism, prayer being made at the same time
> that he may be a partaker of the kingdom of Christ,
> and from Christ can be called a Christian.

After quoting the description of the baptism of Christ from the Gospel, Rabanus continued:

> It is well therefore that in baptism the unction of
> chrism has continued, because the Holy Spirit, who
> through that chrism sanctifies believers with the
> admixture of his power, at Jesus' baptism immediately
> descended upon him in the form of a dove....So it is
> necessary that he who has been baptized should

immediately be succoured with the unction of the chrism, so that, receiving participation in the Holy Spirit, he may not appear alien to Christ.[9]

Rabanus' own rite, like that of the American prayer book, also contained a rite of confirmation to be celebrated at a later time, but it is to the action of the presbyter immediately following baptism that he ascribed the anointing with the Holy Spirit, ascribing to confirmation the gift of boldly proclaiming Christ to others. His position was typical of later medieval thinking about baptism and confirmation, and it retains a measure of influence on contemporary Anglican thought.

Obviously, several intermediate positions are possible. I have espoused such a position myself:

> The pattern of Christian initiation which we find in the [Book of Common Prayer 1979] is of a single sacramental rite which may be administered to either infants or adults. As constituent parts of this rite we find the renunciation of Satan, the confession of faith in the Trinity, Baptism with water into that Name, prayer for the sevenfold Spirit, handlaying, signing with the cross, chrismation, and participation in the Eucharist—all of which we find in the classic rites of the early church. All is described as the Sacrament of Holy Baptism, "full initiation by water and the Holy Spirit into Christ's Body the Church." The sacramental effects are not ascribed to specific moments in the rite, but to the rite as a whole, although the unique central position of the water rite is recognized by the provisions for Emergency Baptism.[10]

My own view is that the outward sign of the inward sealing of the Holy Spirit was the cross marked on the brow of the newly baptized. I identify this sign with "the seal of the living God" with which the angel in Revelation 7:3 "sealed the servants of our God upon their foreheads."[11] This sealing is normatively a part of the complete rite of Christian initiation. There is a wealth of patristic testimony to the significance which the ancient fathers attached to this consignation. Ephraem the Syrian, for example, describes the sign of the cross as the "seal" of the good shepherd imprinted upon his sheep and compares it to a royal signet ring used to impress the king's seal in wax.[12] Chrysostom says that the Evil One cannot stand to look on the cross marked on the foreheads of those who have joined themselves to Christ.[13] Ambrose speaks of God as setting a seal in our hearts and signing us with the image of the cross, so that we may be made like Christ in his passion, rise after his image, and live according to his pattern.[14] Tertullian wrote, "The flesh is signed that the soul too may be protected."[15] A famous third-century epitaph from the catacombs of Callixtus in Rome depicts a dove holding an object resembling a paintbrush in its foot and marking the *chi-rho* monogram.[16] The obvious interpretation is that the Holy Spirit has sealed the departed Christian with the *chi-rho* cross. In this context the fathers generally describe the chrism as the medium with which the seal is applied. It is possible, but by no means certain, that Tertullian, Ambrose, and Augustine knew a consignation made without oil. In any case, it certainly seems that it is the sign of the cross, not the chrism, which is primary to the signing. This is undoubtedly the most reasonable view for Anglicans to take in light of the continued presence of the consignation *without* chrism in the Book of Common Prayer.

It would be most difficult to defend the view that consignation with chrism was a *necessary* part of Christian initiation, both in the light of the official absence of chrismation from Anglican baptismal practice for four centuries and because of the scarcity of New Testament evidence for its use. It has manifestly not been used *semper, ubique, et ab omnibus,* but that does not mean that the tradition is not overwhelmingly in its favor. I believe it would be equally difficult to defend the view that the signing with the cross was itself *necessary,* although it is undoubtedly highly desirable. Emergency baptism has not normally included consignation, indicating that it is not considered an essential part of the rite, but to do sacramental theology by inquiring how little is necessary for validity is seriously to impoverish both liturgy and theology and leads to a dangerous minimalism. Few would contend that the reading and preaching of the Word, for example, was actually *necessary* for the validity of a eucharistic celebration, but even fewer would approve of a rite that did not contain such a proclamation of the Word of God. At the very least, we would consider such a rite seriously defective.

This is my view of the baptismal consignation, and I believe it to be the traditional position of the Anglican Communion. We have consistently defined the baptism "generally necessary to salvation" as being with water in the name of the Trinity, and we have accepted those baptized without consignation as truly baptized, while maintaining the consignation in our own usage and vigorously defending it.

## Chrismation

Chrismation, as I have suggested, has normally been intertwined with consignation through the use of chrism to make the sign of the cross. This usage is officially permitted by the American prayer book and is common, both with and without official authorization, throughout the Anglican Communion. So far as I know, the usage suggested by some ancient texts and medieval Gallican liturgies of an *infusio chrismae*, a pouring of oil over the head of the neophyte separate from the consignation,[17] is not officially practiced in Anglicanism, although I lay no claim to complete knowledge of worldwide Anglican practice.

The prayer for the consecration of the chrism, which immediately follows the thanksgiving over the water in the American baptismal rite, provides a rationale for its use:

> Eternal Father, whose blessed Son was anointed by
> the Holy Spirit to be the Savior and servant of all, we
> pray you to consecrate this oil, that those who are
> sealed with it may share in the royal priesthood of
> Jesus Christ....(BCP 1979, p. 307)

An even fuller statement occurs in *The Book of Occasional Services* authorized by the General Convention of the Episcopal Church in 1979 to supplement the material in the prayer book. It is intended for use when the consecration of chrism takes place apart from baptism:

> In the beginning, the Spirit of God hovered over the creation; and throughout history, God, by the gift of the Holy Spirit, has empowered his people to serve him. As a sign of that gift, the priests and kings of Israel were anointed with oil; and our Lord Jesus Christ was himself anointed at his baptism as the Christ, God's own Messiah. At Baptism Christians are likewise anointed by that same Spirit to empower them for God's service.[18]

The outward anointing with chrism symbolizes the inward anointing with the Holy Spirit and our participation in the *Christos* as members of that "royal priesthood" which is God's new people (1 Pet. 2.9). All Christians at their baptism participate in the messianic anointing of Christ. Christ, of course, was not anointed with oil but with the Holy Spirit (Acts 10.38), and the anointing of Christians is a symbol of that anointing. Some of the fathers speak as if the anointing were itself a second sacramental act intimately united to baptism, so that water and chrism can be spoken of as the two parts of baptism forming a single sacrament just as bread and wine together form the single sacrament of the eucharist. There is much that is attractive in this view, for, among other things, it makes it possible to say that, however desirable it is that both parts of the sacrament be administered together, it is possible to accept what Dix called "baptismal concomitance" and recognize baptism in water without chrismation or consignation as sufficient.

Personally, I find more attractive the suggestion that water baptism and consignation are related in a manner analogous to the anamnetic repetition of the words and acts of Jesus in the eucharist and the eucharistic epiclesis of the Holy Spirit. This makes it clear that we are dealing not with two actions but with different aspects of the same action. The Holy Spirit is active throughout the baptismal action. It is the Spirit who makes it possible for the candidate to confess Jesus Christ as Lord. It is the Spirit who blesses the baptismal water. It is the Spirit who incorporates the baptizand into the dying and rising of Jesus Christ. And it is the Spirit who comes to dwell in the hearts of the neophytes. In the baptismal washing we anamnetically obey the command to baptize. In the post-baptismal chrismation we invoke the indwelling gifts of the Spirit, signing and sealing the new Christian to be Christ's own forever. Some of the patristic writers speak of the Spirit as being given in the baptismal washing itself. John Chrysostom, for example, says,

> The priest makes you go down into the sacred waters, burying the old man and at the same time raising up the new, who is renewed in the image of his Creator. It is at this moment that, through the words and the hand of the priest, the Holy Spirit descends upon you.[19]

The significant thing, I believe, is that all these ancient bishops and theologians were speaking of a single rite: the sacrament of holy baptism. They do not differ about the effects they ascribe to the rite, although some identify particular effects with different parts of the rite, and not necessarily always the same effects with the same ceremony. This is another reason I find the analogy to anamnesis and epiclesis in the eucharist attractive. Theologians differ in attributing eucharistic consecration to different "moments" in the anaphora without necessarily disagreeing about the meaning of the eucharist.

Contemporary eucharistic theologians consider the quest for a "moment of consecration" to be misguided and wish to speak of consecration as being effected by thanksgiving, that is, by the entire eucharistic action, not some particular formula. In the same way, I believe that we should speak of the sacramental effects of baptism, not attempting to ascribe different effects to different parts of the rite. The form for emergency baptism in the American prayer book requires simply the pouring of water with the use of the trinitarian formula, but this is not a proper liturgical rite. It is an answer to the question, "In an emergency, how little is enough?" A rubric clearly provides:

> If the baptized person recovers, the Baptism should be recognized at a public celebration of the Sacrament with a bishop or priest presiding, and the person baptized under emergency conditions, together with the sponsors, taking part in everything except the administration of the water. (BCP 1979, p. 314)

Certainly the promises and the post-baptismal rites are part of the normative baptismal liturgy and are appropriately supplied. Hatchett points out that earlier prayer books did not include the consignation among the rites to be supplied:

> It is significant that, just as in the 1549 rite for Receiving a Child Privately Baptized, the anointing was not supplied (the application of the water with the Trinitarian formula having constituted a full, valid initiation), so in the 1552 Prayer Book this consignation upon the forehead...was not to be supplied. It is made quite clear that such a ceremony is not essential for the completion of baptism, but constitutes an explanation of what has happened at baptism.[20]

The American Book of Common Prayer is not so unambiguous in giving that answer as Hatchett says the earlier books were, but there can be no doubt that the central point remains valid. The Episcopal Church does, in fact, explicitly permit deacons to preside at public baptisms on major baptismal feasts and with the bishop's special authorization, and it directs the deacons to omit the prayer for the gifts of the Spirit and the consignation, thereby affirming that these actions are reserved to priests and bishops (BCP 1979, p. 312). It permits, *but does not require*, the omitted action to be supplied at a subsequent celebration of baptism at which a bishop or priest presides.

The conclusion I would draw from all this is that the baptismal washing is of the very essence of baptism. Without it we are simply not talking about baptism. The post-baptismal consignation is a significant rite integral to the proper celebration of the sacrament, but not so necessary that it must at all costs be supplied, if it has been omitted, although the American prayer book leans heavily toward supplying it. The American prayer book also considers it to be a sacerdotal act, restricting it to bishops and priests, while permitting deacons to administer the water baptism in the public rite. This, of course, need mean nothing more than that the tradition of the ancient liturgies is being followed, which does not necessarily mean that the theological implications have been thought through. It does mean, however, that the intention is to follow the tradition of the church, not to innovate.

The use of chrism for the consignation is much more controversial. Many Episcopalians, like other Anglicans, wish that chrism were always used for the consignation. I include myself among them. Others, seeing no clear evidence for its use in the New Testament, nor a unanimous tradition in the church throughout its history, prefer not to introduce it, and I do not see how an Anglican can consistently hold that chrismation is necessary.

## Confirmation

Although I have chosen to discuss the question in terms of the meaning of consignation and chrismation, this is not the usual focus of theological discussion about the initiation rites of the Episcopal Church. That discussion has tended to turn upon the question of whether the post-baptismal consignation is not more properly called confirmation. Certainly it appears to be the rite which J. D. C. Fisher[21] and (in a somewhat different way) Gregory Dix[22] call confirmation. It is certainly not what G. W. H. Lampe[23] considers confirmation to be, and the rite of confirmation in the

American prayer book is much closer to Lampe's view than to that of Dix. I have suggested this discussion resembles in many ways an Anglo-American discussion of football that involves, not substantial questions concerning the game, but which of the games called by that name is correctly so designated. In the absence of agreed definitions, the conversation may prove difficult, but once the nomenclature is understood on all sides, a substantive discussion is perfectly possible.

What the Episcopal Church believes it has achieved is a common rite that all will agree is "full initiation by water and the Holy Spirit into Christ's Body the Church." Anglicans have frequently disagreed about the precise theological interpretations of their rites, but have been united in their common use of them.

## Wider Implications

Underlying all this discussion is the belief that baptism and eucharist are unique as Gospel sacraments of the passion and resurrection of Jesus Christ, and that their common proclamation of our participation in the paschal mystery of Christ's death and resurrection relates them to each other. They have always occupied a special place in Anglican sacramental theology as "generally necessary to salvation." The implication is that one who has been baptized is a communicant and should be communicating. There are many reasons why this is not actually the case, but the only proper reasons for refusing communion to baptized persons is open and notorious evil life, i.e., public excommunication. Age has not generally been seen as a proper impediment, and many would urge the theological propriety of communicating those being baptized at their baptism, regardless of their age, pointing to the long-standing tradition of both East and West in favor of so doing.[24]

Certainly it was the intention of the Episcopal Church, or at least of those who drafted the initiation rites for the prayer book, to provide a rite that would make the connection between baptism and eucharist explicit. Other churches might wish to quibble about the need for confirmation, although the Lambeth Conference in 1968 recommended alternative practices concerning confirmation and admission to communion,[25] including communion at an early age. It is here suggested that a baptismal rite containing post-baptismal consignation, as Anglican rites have since the sixteenth century, should be considered complete, and there is no need to consider any rite which includes water baptism in the name of the Trinity to be so essentially defective that those baptized with it are ineligible to communicate.

## Notes

1. An English translation of the Gelasian form of the prayer appears in E. C. Whitaker, *Documents of the Baptismal Liturgy* (London: SPCK, 1970), p. 88, n. 95. The Latin text is in *Liber Sacramentorum Romanae Ecclesiae Ordinis Anni Circuli (Sacramentarium Gelasianum)*, ed. L. C. Mohlberg (Rome: Herder, 1960), p. 74, n. 450.

2. Examples may be found in Whitaker, *Documents*, pp. 121 (the Mozarabic *Liber Ordinum*), 162 *(Missale Gothicum)*, and 152 (the Ambrosian *Beroldus*).

3. The source is clearly the Mozarabic *Missale Mixtum*. See F. E. Brightman, *The English Rite* (London: Rivingtons, 1921), 2:738-40, English translation in J. D. C. Fisher, *Christian Initiation: The Reformation Period*, Alcuin Club Collections 51 (London: SPCK, 1970), pp. 151-53.

4. The classic Anglican defense of the cross in baptism is in Richard Hooker, *Of the Laws of Ecclesiastical Polity*, Book 5, lxv.

5. The form is found in all Anglican prayer books from 1552 until the present round of revisions.

6. Marion Hatchett, "The Rite of 'Confirmation' in the Book of Common Prayer and in *Authorized Services 1973*," *Anglican Theological Review* 56 (1974): 296.

7. (London: Longmans, Green, 1951); 2nd ed. (London: SPCK, 1967).

8. (Westminster: Dacre, 1946).

9. Quoted in J. D. C. Fisher, *Christian Initiation: Baptism in the Medieval West*, Alcuin Club Collections 47 (London: SPCK, 1965), p. 63.

10. Leonel L. Mitchell, "The Theology of Christian Initiation and *The Proposed Book of Common Prayer*," *Anglican Theological Review* 60 (1978): 418.

11. Although Revelation does not specify that the seal was the sign of the cross, the parallel with Ezekiel 9:4, in which a *taw* was marked on the foreheads of those who sigh and groan over the abominations committed in Jerusalem, certainly suggests that the seal was in the form of an X or +. See Leonel L. Mitchell, *Baptismal Anointing* (Notre Dame, Ind.: University of Notre Dame Press, 1978), pp. 19f, 24.

12. Mitchell, *Baptismal Anointing*, p. 35.

13. Whitaker, *Documents*, p. 37.

14. *De sacramentis* 6.2; see Mitchell, *Baptismal Anointing*, p. 89.

15. *De resurrectione carnis* 8; see Whitaker, *Documents*, p. 10.

16. Cyril E. Pocknee, *Cross and Crucifix*, Alcuin Club Tracts 32 (London: Mowbray, 1962), p. 17, plate I.

17. The phrase is from *Missale Gallicanum Vetus*, ed. L. C. Mohlberg (Rome: Herder, 1958), p. 67, n. 260.

18. *The Book of Occasional Services* (New York: Church Hymnal Corporation, 1979), p. 210.

19. Stavronikita Series, 2. 25; *St. John Chrysostom: Baptismal Instructions*, trans. Paul W. Harkins, Ancient Christian Writers 31 (Westminster, Md.: Newman, 1963), p. 52; quoted also in Whitaker, *Documents*, p. 40.

20. Hatchett, "The Rite of 'Confirmation,'" p. 306.

21. J. D. C. Fisher, "History and Theology," in *Crisis for*

*Confirmation*, ed. Michael Perry (London: SCM, 1967); cf. the US version, *Confirmation Crisis* (New York: Seabury, 1968), pp. 19-42.

22. Gregory Dix, *Confirmation or the Laying on of Hands?* Theology Occasional Papers 5 (London: SCM, 1936).

23. *Seal of the Spirit*, p. 314.

24. See J. D. C. Fisher, "The Separation of Communion from Initiation," in *Christian Initiation: Baptism in the Medieval West*, pp. 101-8.

25. Lambeth suggested either that baptized children be admitted to Holy Communion at an "appropriate" age and confirmation deferred, or that infant baptism and confirmation be administered together, with admission to Holy Communion at "an early age," and a "commissioning for service" by the bishop be added when the person was capable of making a responsible commitment (Lambeth Conference 1968, *Resolutions and Reports* [London: SPCK; New York: Seabury, 1968], p. 99). It has not been entirely clear to many people which alternative the Episcopal Church followed, but it can be suggested, not unreasonably, that Lambeth's alternatives are not different practices but different ways of describing the same practice.

# American Perspectives: (ii) Confirmation

*Louis Weil*

In the United States, confirmation has been very much linked with the distinctive identity of Anglicans. In other words, for a great many, either consciously or unconsciously, it is the sign of becoming a member of the Episcopal Church. The reason for this is rather simple. A significant percentage of the membership of the Episcopal Church have come into Anglicanism from other Christian (and non-Christian) backgrounds. Early in the history of the Episcopal Church, confirmation emerged as the sign, in a country profoundly affected by frontier Protestant religious values, of membership in a religious tradition which understood itself as part of a more comprehensive vision of the church, both historically and geographically. At the same time, it was recognized that within American culture, in which the Episcopal Church found itself in the midst of various denominations which rejected the practice of confirmation, a biblical foundation had to be asserted for such a sign. Consequently Acts 8.14-17 was inserted into the confirmation rite for the first time in the 1892 BCP, thus providing within the context of the rite evidence that the practice rested upon biblical authority. In his commentary on the American BCP of 1928, the late Massey H. Shepherd comments:

> The lesson should not be interpreted strictly to imply
> that the Holy Spirit has not been imparted to those
> who have been baptized in His Name and incorporat-

ed into the fellowship of His love; but that in this rite, which stems from the practice of the apostles, the graces of the Holy Spirit are given and assured in a new and special sense.[1]

This perspective to confirmation and its acceptance as a normal prerequisite to full church membership (and, by implication, to communion) was generally taken for granted. The rubric written by Archbishop John Peckham of Canterbury in the thirteenth century offered an authoritative framework to the view that confirmation must normally precede communion. Little historical awareness came into play in all of this, and even the early stages of liturgical study seemed to support the idea that Anglicanism had providentially preserved the "primitive order": baptism, confirmation, communion.

Other perspectives emerged as study of the rites of initiation deepened, perspectives which are now easily accessible to anyone willing to do some study on the history of those rites, and specifically on the itinerant evolution of what is known as confirmation within the Anglican tradition. Among the many aspects of this matter, perhaps most important has been the realization that in our tradition two basic and quite distinct strands of meaning came together in what we call "confirmation" and that the result was really something of a muddle. Years ago, the late Urban T. Holmes said to me that confirmation is rather like Humpty-Dumpty, and that we could not simply reverse history and put the pieces back together again. We carry our history, and pastoral practice has been shaped from within this muddle, this undistinguished blending of two elements: the concluding episcopal rite of the primitive, integrated pattern, and the Reformation rite of an owning of the faith by one who had been baptized as a child and who had now reached "maturity" (according to some definition).

The subcommittee of the Standing Liturgical Commission which was charged with the task of preparing the revision of these rites for the 1979 Book of Common Prayer, attempted to face this history with the best knowledge available today, both historical and theological, and with a realistic approach to the inherited pastoral attitudes. This means, of course, that a time of transition at the level of practice would be inevitable, but that at the same time recent pastoral models could not enslave us to a pattern which was suspect on the basis of solid historical and theological reflection. A major example of the latter was the issue of the communion of infants. Historical research clearly demonstrated that for many centuries the communion of infants had followed directly upon baptism, and that the breakdown of the practice was not based upon any idea (at first) of the unsuitability of infants as recipients of the eucharistic gifts, but rather to the widespread defection of the laity in general from communion. Theological reflection pointed out the anomaly of a break between the rite of incorporation and the sign of incorporation.

Such study, however, was the concern of a rather small elite and had rather little impact on the general norms of pastoral practice. In the late 1960s, there were some experiments in a few dioceses of the Episcopal Church with "early" admission to communion, but this applied to children rather than to infants. These instances do indicate that a certain shift in attitude was taking place prior to the action of the General Convention in 1970, and may well have contributed to an enlarged awareness of the issue at least among some delegates to the convention. For the great majority of Episcopalians, however, those who were charged with the development of the new rite seemed to be introducing into the Episcopal Church a strange innovation, foreign to the prayer book tradition and to commonly accepted practice. They were, in effect, asking the Episcopal Church to change its mind, and this was met by both confusion and rejection. Behind the proposed change, however, lay a very practical consideration based upon pastoral experience, that is, that confirmation as generally practiced simply was not working. The high percentage of people who fell away from regular participation in the life of the church *after* confirmation served as a clear indication that drastic change was needed.

This pastoral awareness was complemented by the impact of the recovery of deeper historical insight as it reached the more popular levels of Christian reflection. The historical perspective suddenly made it clear that what had come to be experienced as distinct sacramental acts, albeit in their primitive order, were dependent upon their essential unity in the experience of Christians if their meaning was not to be undermined. Compartmentalization of the three actions had led to a detrimental modification of the theology of initiation. To a significant degree, the separation of the three actions in the Middle Ages accompanied a loss of an ecclesial sense of all sacramental actions in the church, that is, that it is the whole church which is involved in the sacraments.

The corporate dimension was progressively obscured in the medieval period as concern focussed increasingly on the grace which the *individual* receives in a sacrament. There was a loss of the sense that grace is first of all God's gift to the whole body of the church and then derivatively a particularization in individual believers. It is no surprise that the public worship of the church during this evolution came to be the explicit domain of the ordained clergy, almost as private clerical acts to which the laity had passive access through a piety of vision. This understanding of liturgy and sacraments came in recent years to be seen as radically foreign to the mind of the church during the early centuries. Thus historical insight and the awareness of contemporary failure combined to create an imperative for change.

The first practical fruit of this imperative is found in the action of the General Convention of 1970 in authorizing the initiatory rite of *Prayer Book Studies 18* for trial use. In the provisions attached to the authorization of the rite, it was stated that children should "be admitted to Holy Communion before Confirmation, subject to the direction and guidance of the Ordinary."[2] Through this action the convention had restored in principle the ancient unity between the first reception of communion and baptism. A year later, the House of Bishops issued a document known as the "Pocono Statement" in which the implications of this directive with regard to the understanding of confirmation were stated explicitly: "Confirmation should not be regarded as a procedure of admission to the Holy Communion."[3] Critics responded that the "primitive order" which Anglicanism providentially preserved had now been shattered. Yet historical reflection on the twofold heritage of confirmation in Anglicanism does not permit this misreading of the tradition.

The commission which developed the new rite of the 1979 Book of Common Prayer wanted to make clear that communion was the final initiatory act of incorporation into the body of Christ, and that the new rite should express what is generally believed to have been Archbishop Cranmer's intention, namely, that "Holy Baptism is full initiation by water and the Holy Spirit into Christ's Body the Church" (BCP, p. 298), and that this rite itself incorporated the signing with a cross on the forehead which in early centuries was performed by the bishop after the water rite and prior to communion. In a preliminary version of the new rite, the committee included a rubric which indicated that "Those who have now been baptized may receive Holy Communion,"[4] but this was later eliminated by the Standing Liturgical Commission, perhaps because it seemed to press the issue too urgently. In spite of that loss, however, the fact that the principal Sunday eucharist is established as the normative context for the celebration of baptism in the new rite is a potent argument for the fulfillment of the initiatory act in the reception of the eucharistic gifts by the newly baptized.

The Pocono Statement broke the link between confirmation and the reception of communion, and paved the way to a stronger case for the interpretation of confirmation within Anglicanism as a rite of mature affirmation of faith in the presence of the bishop and sealed by the laying on of hands, rather than as a disconnected part of the initiatory process. That view, in turn, encourages the reclaiming of the signing in baptism in its primitive sense, as an auxiliary articulation of the essential meaning of the water rite.

That view is supported by the fact that the bishop, when present, says the prayer for the gifts of the Holy Spirit and performs the signing. In the bishop's absence, this part of the sacramental sequence is performed by the priest, as is generally typical given the pastoral realities of our time. The bishop cannot be present for all baptisms, but The Book of Common Prayer indirectly suggests in the wording of the second rubric before the confirmation rite (p. 412) that adult baptisms take place with the bishop present. Whether the signing be done by bishop or priest, the permitted use of the consecrated oil of chrism is a further indication of the influence of the primitive norm upon the new rite.

The question of the communion of infants must thus be seen within the wider theological context of the relation of communion to the initiatory pattern. After the House of Bishops issued the Pocono Statement, a great deal of debate ensued as to the age at which unconfirmed children might receive communion. Given past pastoral practice, this initial approach was probably inevitable, but it poses the question the wrong way around, and there is an arbitrary character to all the various ages which have been proposed. If we ask, rather, at what age the baptized may receive communion, the mind of the church of the early centuries, when the initiatory process was a single whole, is that communion is the *right* of the baptized by virtue of their incorporation into Christ. Only willful sin inhibits that right, and infants are the primary example of persons of whom such sin is not characteristic.

If we hold to the integrity of the initiatory pattern in this way, Anglican confirmation emerges as a pastoral rite, not as a prerequisite to communion. It is an occasion when, as the first confirmation rubric indicates, "those baptized at an early age are expected, when they are ready and have been duly prepared, to make a mature public affirmation of their faith and commitment to the responsibilities of their Baptism and to receive the laying on of hands by the bishop" (BCP, p. 412). Confirmation is thus related to the church's ministry in the fostering of maturity in the

Christian life and of preparation for the profession of one's faith within the context of the church's corporate sacramental life. If this seems to put confirmation in its place, it is not a place of minor importance in the church's life, and yet it is made clear that its role is as a pastoral complement to the practice of infant baptism and not a theological rival to the fundamental sacramental sign in which the Christian life begins.

On a Sunday in Eastertide in the spring of 1985, it was my privilege to preach at the principal liturgy in the cathedral of a New England diocese of the Episcopal Church. At that liturgy, the infant son of a committed young couple was baptized and then was anointed by the diocesan bishop. Later, in that same liturgy, the bishop gave the eucharistic gifts to the newly-baptized as he was held in the arms of one of his parents. What struck me with overwhelming power in this liturgy was the unselfconsciousness of these acts on the part of the community gathered that day. It was perceived as natural, as what *should* be done.

Although this model cannot be claimed as common throughout the Episcopal Church at this time, the number of young baptized children who have, by virtue of their baptism, received communion and who are regular participants by virtue of the commitment of their parents is increasing. One is tempted to read this issue in terms of one's own experience, and for fourteen years I have lived in a seminary community in which the communion of infants is a normal part of our sacramental life. Yet we all know that a seminary is not a parish or mission, nor can its liturgical norms be taken as typical of the wider worshiping community. A seminary is a place where education and socialization occur at a considerably faster rate than is possible in a parish. Issues may be addressed and discussed in depth because a resident community is involved in an intensity of day-to-day contact which is not characteristic of parochial models.

Yet there is evidence that where the issue of the relation of communion to baptism in regard to young children has been raised, there is a generally positive response to a modification of past practice and an acceptance of the idea that confirmation is not a barrier to be crossed before communion may be received. Emerging models show a rather rapid assimilation of the implications of "full initiation" into the body of Christ.

## Notes

1. *The Oxford American Prayer Book Commentary* (New York: Oxford, 1950), commentary on p. 296.

2. *Services for Trial Use* (New York: Church Hymnal Corporation, 1971), p. 21.

3. Report of the Special Meeting of the House of Bishops, 1971, in *Journal of the General Convention of...the Episcopal Church*, 1973, p. 1073.

4. *Holy Baptism, together with A Form for Confirmation or the Laying On of Hands by the Bishop with the Affirmation of Baptismal Vows*, Prayer Book Studies 26 (New York: Church Hymnal Corporation, 1973), pp. 16, 18, 19.

# 7

# American Perspectives: (iii) Mystagogia

*Robert J. Brooks*

The past ten years have seen a rapidly developing scholarly consensus on the nature of Christian initiation. Insights have
come from diverse disciplines such as scripture studies, theology,
history, psychology, anthropology, and Christian education. Added
to the contribution of scholarship has been the experience of
revised rites of initiation in parishes throughout the Anglican
Communion. The scholarly convergence and pastoral witness have
combined increasingly to point to the need to articulate a norm
that baptism admits to communion and that the eucharist is the
right of all the baptized, regardless of age.

The Boston Statement articulates a catechetical principle
derived from the early church that baptism into the death and resurrection of Jesus Christ opens up a whole lifetime of unfolding
the rich meaning of what has already been given in the sacrament.
This continual process was known in the early church as "mystagogia." Because of the mystagogical milieu of patristic communities, our contemporary questions, such as, "How can you give
communion to *infants* or small *children* when they do not understand it?" or "How do we provide for *adult* education?" would
have puzzled our ancestors in the faith. Their question was, "How
does our communal life draw on and manifest the meaning of
what was given in baptism for the faithful of all ages?" Children,
adults, people of all ages, are nurtured in communion. The Boston
Statement discountenances any requirement of a minimum age or
understanding for admission to communion, as "the whole church,

by celebrating baptism and eucharist, and by practicing everything else which builds up the community, proclaims the meaning of its baptismal life and affirms its being as a community of Christian faith which transcends boundaries of understanding, differences of temperament, and varieties of gifts within the one body." This mystagogical methodology contrasts with the inherited Enlightenment pattern which influenced previous Anglican catechetical practice but has now been philosophically discredited.

A false issue has been made of the relation of catechesis to children and communion. The question for infants and younger children is not, "How do they receive catechesis before baptism?" but "How do all the baptized continually experience mystagogia throughout their post-baptismal life?" The methodology of the early church and of the Boston Statement—"experience first, then reflect"—has special relevance to younger children. As Heidegger has shown, in order for understanding to take place, there must be a pre-understanding of the subject. A child who, as Massey Shepherd said, "can never remember a time when he or she did not receive communion," will have an experience from the day of baptism that provides the pre-understanding necessary for obtaining meaning. The unfolding of meaning becomes a lifelong process of assimilating the richness of the gift of God's grace. One does not attain this by the "work" of understanding the gift. It is rather a matter of "standing under" the awesome gift of grace. A lifetime becomes a continual dialogue between the affective experience of communion from the day of baptism and cognitive reflection on that experience. That is mystagogia.

The major objection to children receiving communion, whether it comes from clergy or laity, is, "They should not take communion until they understand it." This argument has been dominant because of the assumptions of the Age of Reason inaugurated by the Enlightenment which would really define understanding as "overstanding." Knowledge was seen as a limited, exhaustible field of information. It was thought possible to stand outside of history and culture in a detached, objective manner, allowing for a "standing over" any subject matter to grasp all the information until none was left. Frequently, the actual experience of confirmation instruction was that those confirmed believed that they had learned everything necessary about Christianity since they would not have been confirmed if they did not know and understand it all. Unfortunately, knowing the seasons of the church year might not have been of great guidance or comfort when a marriage disintegrated or one was faced with extended layoff from employment. The experience of acceptance and meaning in a eucharistic community might be more sustaining.

The Enlightenment notion of understanding has been effectively shattered by the work of Martin Heidegger. As previously noted, his concept of pre-understanding undermines the possibility of objective distancing from a subject. Hans-Georg Gadamer has shown that we stand in the river of history so that our values, our methods of analysis, etc., form our very ability to understand any subject. We cannot step outside of history into some abstract objectivity. Understanding is a process of formation and dialogue, not of apprehending information in a one-way conversation with the subject. This understanding is usually expressed in our current debate as, "How can we deprive children of the eucharist until they understand it? No one, clergy and theologians included, understands it." From a theological viewpoint, this insight of Heidegger and Gadamer can point us back to the affirmation of God as mystery and of symbols as multivalent, inexhaustible sources of meaning. Mystery and symbol drive us to true understanding—not Enlightenment "overstanding," but Christian "standing under."

Free of Enlightenment hubris, the whole of baptismal life, whenever it begins, can be seen as mystagogia. We will realize that all of the arguments for or against baptism are really the same arguments as those for and against infant communion. Since we do not wait to feed infants or children until they understand nutrition, we should not wait to give communion to baptized infants or children until they "understand" the eucharist.

If there is no longer any philosophical basis for depriving children of communion, it would be well to consider what might be the principal elements of a mystagogic community for all the baptized. These elements will be drawn from reflection on ten years of personal experience with a parish in which all the baptized, regardless of age, received the eucharist. This personal reflection will help to illustrate the suggested pattern for communal initiatory life in the pastoral section of the Boston Statement.

Such a pattern presumes the recognition that mystagogia is central to the lifestyle of the baptized. In baptism, we are fully initiated into the Christian community. It takes one's whole life to assimilate the meaning of what it is to be initiated into the Crucified and Risen One. The baptismal life is a process of unfolding meaning in a dialogue with the particular events of life and the Christian story. A baptized person is not an empty vessel that is filled from time to time with information during first communion classes, confirmation classes, adult or Lenten study groups. In baptism, the paschal mystery has taken flesh in a person. One is filled with that life. A mystagogic community evokes from the person the richness and diversity of meaning already present within.

This mystagogical milieu is constant within the liturgical assembly. The liturgy of the word is a storytelling rite which is a mirror to us of who we are. John the Deacon, in his letter to a Roman nobleman in 500 C.E., said that baptism tells us, "who we are and who we are becoming." The liturgy of the word is an epiphany through story of who God is and who we are, transfiguring us more and more into the image of God made manifest in our baptism. The Sunday lectionary, year in and year out, is the curriculum of our mystagogia. However much we may need to turn and repent, we always do so as those who are already baptized, as those who must "become who you are," as St. Augustine said. Besides the symbol of story, other symbols such as meal, water, oil, hands, body, by the way they are used over and over in liturgy, have a disclosive power about God and ourselves. When baptism looks like bathing/drowning, when eucharist looks like meal, the situation of our own life and that of the community is drawn out by those open symbols to proclaim new meaning and reveal the paschal passage in the lives of the baptized. The seasons of the church year concentrate us on certain elements of the meaning of our baptismal life. Regular opportunities to renew our baptismal covenant enable us to hear ourselves saying "yes" again to the inexhaustible meaning of our baptism. That renewal is a part of mystagogia itself.

Certain significant times in life enable mystagogical catechesis to evoke meaning for the baptized person in those events. Some of these key times would be entering adult responsibility, taking or retaking vocation, marriage, reconciliation, sickness, death. As a person is going through change in these moments, mystagogia would relate the person's passage into changed circumstances to Jesus' exodus from death to life into which that person was baptized.

The presence of catechumens in baptismal communities also acts as a catalyst to evoke meaning of the dignity and destiny of the already baptized. In a sense, catechumens are the most effective mystagogues of the baptized. They personalize and embody in their diverse personalities and in the richness of each one's personhood, the diversity and richness of meaning of the baptismal life.

I have taken time to describe a mystagogic community because the notion of how children are nurtured in communion needs to be seen within this context. They should not be treated separately from the mystagogical norm of all the baptized. Now we can consider elements of mystagogia for infants and children.

The first concerns the formation of the parents as sponsors for children to be baptized. As sponsors, the parents represent the catechetical mystagogical responsibility of the whole community in the home, the domestic church. By their baptismal lifestyle the parents will speak volumes about the Christian faith to their children and can be more intimate sponsors than anyone else in the parish. In reflecting on sponsoring their own children, it is useful to have sessions with other parents in the parish so that a dialogue can begin about the experiences of sponsoring children. Sharing of stories by other parents is illuminating to new parent sponsors. Parents will discover that God is acting in their lives through the gift of children and that new dimensions of their own baptismal ministry have opened up. Their formation for sponsorship is mystagogia that facilitates assimilation of new meaning of their baptismal call. The new child is born into a faith community both at home and in the church ready to initiate it into that faith.

The community itself is also formed as sponsor and mystagogue for infants and children. As mentioned previously here and in the Boston Statement, the celebration of the liturgy itself expresses meaning for the baptismal life. Children experience time (baptismal days, Sundays) and the material universe (water, oil, bread, wine, body) as sacraments of God. The diversity of ministries in the liturgy manifests the richness of God's call to humanity. Children learn by playing and the liturgy enables us to play God's reign in our midst. They enter into the story and symbolic action freely and without affectation. In fact, they have a baptismal ministry that they exercise to the community. They opened the eyes of many an adult in my parish to see the joy of the eucharist as well as to relate the grace before meals at home to the eucharistic prayer at church. Too often we arrogantly think that catechesis for children is one-way. One could ask, "Who is being catechized?"

The community acts as mystagogue for children especially through baptism. Children who witness baptisms of those of all ages year in and year out grow up in a community that constantly manifests the richness of their own baptismal mystery. Each occasion is mystagogical in itself, revealing new dimensions.

The Boston Statement has detailed the implications for admitting children to communion that have resulted from scholarly consensus. It invites the Anglican Communion to nurture its children in communion in mystagogical communities of baptismal faith and life. Let us get on with the mission of manifesting those communities.

# 8

# New Zealand Initiation Experience: (i) A Changing Initiatory Pattern

Brian Davis

Prior to 1970 the initiation pattern in New Zealand was generally baptism in infancy, confirmation in the early teens, followed by admission to communion. By the late 1960s clergy had begun to question "indiscriminate" baptismal practices and were introducing pre-baptismal instruction for parents and encouraging baptism at the main mid-morning eucharist. At the same time concerns were being expressed about confirmation theology and practice. Confirmation was understood as a "completion of baptism." More often than not it seemed to be a "passing-out parade" from active involvement in the life of the church.

A spur to initiation reform was the increasing secularization of society and the desire among clergy to encourage a more intentional and disciplined membership. The more immediate stimulus for reform was the lead given by the Lambeth bishops in 1968. Lambeth recommended "that each province or regional church be asked to explore the theology of baptism and confirmation in relation to the need to commission laity for their task in the world, and to experiment in this regard."[1]

The climate that made change possible was increasing frustration and unease, especially among clergy, with the "traditional" initiation practice. There were a number of concerns:

1. Throughout the church universal there seemed to be a growing consensus that baptism admits one to full membership in

the body of Christ. The consequence of this seemed to be that baptism and baptism alone was the sacramental requirement for admission to communion.

2. If baptism was the sacrament of membership it was felt that it should be administered with greater care and that parents and the church should take more seriously the responsibility for the nurture of baptized children to mature commitment in Christ.

3. Confirmation could not be the sacrament of "full membership" nor should it be seen as giving the necessary "ticket to communion." Confirmation provided an opportunity for a responsible (adult) faith affirmation. The laying-on-of-hands and prayer could best be understood as a "commissioning" for lay ministry.

4. Educators were beginning to provide a clearer understanding of how children grow in the faith, of the significance of symbolic actions, and of the young child's sense of wonder and mystery.[2] Too much emphasis, it was said, had been put on propositional or conceptual teaching with the children separate from the worshiping fellowship. The value of teaching the faith through involvement of children in the sacramental community of faith was being rediscovered.

From 1970 the Provincial Board of Christian Education began a series of annual provincial consultations to give direction to initiation experimentation in the province. Those promoting reform had three particular expectations:

1. That parents seeking baptism for their children would have a clear understanding of the sacrament, including its essential ecclesial character, and be ready to fulfill the responsibilities it brings.

2. That children admitted to holy communion earlier would benefit from sharing the sacrament with the family and enjoy an experience of worship that would form a sound basis for

later conceptual learning and involvement in the life of the church.

3. That those seeking confirmation would be ready to make a responsible commitment to follow Christ and be commissioned for Christian service in the world.

## General Synod Authorization

General Synod in 1970 agreed to permit dioceses to experiment along the lines of the Lambeth resolution and in 1972 recommended the following pattern:

(i) Baptism from infancy.

(ii) Provision for admission to communion prior to confirmation.

(iii) Confirmation as an event of adult life.

The Synod further resolved that "those admitted to Holy Communion prior to confirmation must be accepted as communicant throughout the Province."

The 1976 General Synod recognized the pattern above as "an alternative practice" and approved "Guidelines" drawn up by the Provincial Board of Christian Education. The guidelines stated "that at least one parent or guardian must desire baptism for the child and show this by becoming a sponsor...bring the child up as a member of the Christian community participating in the education, worship and fellowship of the parish." Children could be admitted to communion "at not less than eight years of age...after at least one year's regular participation in the worshiping and/or educational life of the Church." There would be appropriate instruction prior to the special service of admission, and names would be entered in a diocesan register. Candidates for confirmation would "normally be 16 years of age or over...ready to affirm their faith and be commissioned for their ministry as responsible Christians in the world."

General Synod in 1978 reaffirmed the "alternative practice" by resolution, but its legality was challenged by an appeal to the

Supreme Court. The appellants claimed that the "alternative practice" was in conflict with the confirmation rubric in the Book of Common Prayer, i.e., "there shall none be admitted to Holy Communion until such time as he be confirmed, or be ready and desirous to be confirmed." The Supreme Court ruled that the matter should be first considered by an appropriate church court, this being the Judicial Committee.

The Judicial Committee decided that the confirmation rubric did not permit the "alternative initiation practice," and a special General Synod was called in 1979 to make the necessary legislative changes. The resulting canon stated:

1. Not withstanding the provisions of the rubrics relating to Admission to Holy Communion it shall be permitted as an alternative practice in the Church of the Province of New Zealand for Baptized children to be admitted to Holy Communion prior to Confirmation after instruction approved by the Bishop.

2. The General Synod may from time to time approve Guidelines which shall be followed in administering the alternative practice.

3. Those admitted to Holy Communion under the provisions of this Canon shall not be eligible to take any office where communicant status is mandatory unless they also shall have been confirmed.[3]

Under the Empowering Act procedure this legislation was ratified at the 1980 session of General Synod, and Synod approved revised guidelines. These guidelines were made "Standing Resolutions" in 1982.

The significant changes between the 1976 guidelines and those of 1980 were:

1. The 1980 guidelines incorporated both the traditional and new initiation practices.

2. No lower age limit for admission to communion was stated. Admission can take place when "the family and parish priest

judge appropriate, *or* after more formal instruction and at a special service, *or* after laying-on-of-hands by the Bishop following instruction." (The reference in the canon to admission "after instruction approved by the Bishop" would appear to rule out infant communion at present.)

3. No lower age limit was mentioned for confirmation, but candidates "will be ready to affirm their faith and to be commissioned for their ministry as responsible Christians in the world."

4. Chrismation was made optional at both the baptism of adults and the baptism of children.

"Pastoral Notes" were added to the guidelines related to baptism, admission to communion and confirmation practice. Under "Admission of Children to Communion," the pastoral notes refer to the value of parents participating in the instruction and the need for the congregation to "recognize" the admission when this happens informally.

In the report to General Synod from the 1980 Provincial Consultation responsible for revising the guidelines, the following statement was made:

> There is now emerging a consensus in the Western Church on a number of issues:
>
> 1. Baptism is full initiation by water and the Spirit into Christ's body, the Church, whether received by an adult or a child. (In the words of the Catechism, baptism makes a person "a member of Christ, the Child of God, and an inheritor of the kingdom of heaven.") Commitment to such a position implies a disciplined practice for the baptism of children.
>
> 2. There is no support in the New Testament or in the early tradition of the church for a distinction between the baptized community and the eucharistic community. Nor is there any support for a distinction between membership and full membership.

3. The fullness of baptism may be more adequately expressed by an act of chrismation (the anointing with oil consecrated by the bishop). The present consignation (signing with the cross) is in fact a vestige of an anointing omitted from the Prayer Book of 1552.

4. The laying-on-of-hands by the bishop may be understood as the commissioning of adults for service and witness within the church and the world.

5. Baptized children may be admitted to communion prior to the laying-on-of-hands by the bishop.

6. Persons baptized in childhood need the opportunity to affirm their baptismal vows. This takes place at the laying-on-of-hands by the bishop, and/or at some previous time.

The church is not yet in a position to give a final or common answer to all the questions that arise from the practice of Christian initiation. The difficulty is that within the Anglican Communion and the wider church, new pastoral and liturgical practices are developing at different paces. We need to allow the Holy Spirit room to lead us into truth, within guidelines that define the outer limits of a practice faithful to the biblical witness.

The revised Provincial Guidelines have been prepared bearing in mind these factors and provide for the continuation of "traditional" as well as alternative practices.

It is the considered view of the Provincial Board of Christian Education that at this stage, the Church will be better served by a set of guidelines rather than by a definitive Canon as suggested by the special session of General Synod.

The guidelines allow the flexibility necessary for each

diocese to move as it believes the Holy Spirit is leading, and yet consistent with the emerging consensus within the Western Church.

They will also give guidance for the Provincial Commission on Prayer Book Revision as it seeks to provide for the liturgical needs of the Church in the area of Christian initiation.

The guidelines are offered in a generous spirit and will require charity and goodwill among the dioceses of the Province.[4]

Dioceses have been free to apply the alternative practice according to their own requirements, consistent with the provincial guidelines. Several dioceses have produced their own expanded guidelines.

## Evaluation

It is clear that a change of initiation practice brings far-reaching pastoral, liturgical and educational implications, not always fully understood by clergy and lay parish leaders.

Parishes have found it necessary to review their educational program as a result of admitting children to communion. Some typical models adopted include:

1. A weekday Church School with children free to attend worship with parents on Sunday.

2. A Sunday Church School at the same time (or starting shortly before) the main Eucharist, with children having their own "Ministry of the Word" and returning to join their parents at the Offertory.

3. A brief time of instruction (five minutes) for the children in the context of the liturgy, and possibly some activity for the youngest children during the worship.

The presence of younger children at worship has encouraged a rethinking of church design and furnishings. Wall-to-wall carpeting has become increasingly popular, or at least a carpeted space for young children to play on. Chairs tend to be replacing pews.

Banners, drama, dance and instrumental music provide added interest for children, and they are encouraged to share in the worship as servers, readers, intercessors, dancers, etc.

A recent questionnaire used with children who have been admitted to communion and their parents indicated that children appreciated receiving communion earlier because it made them feel that "they belonged" and were an integral part of "God's family." Responses revealed that the children experienced through their involvement in the eucharist "nearness to God," encouragement, acceptance, strength and wholeness.

Many parents commented on the importance of the sense of belonging and acceptance by admission of children to communion. Some found it easier to be a family together at worship than send their children to Sunday School. One parent summed up the experience of many when she said, "To enjoy the service fully with the children is an added joy to the act of communion itself. I believe the early admission to communion is working well."

## Age of Admission

Although the 1980 provincial guidelines left the question of the age for admission to communion open, most dioceses adopted a policy of admitting children at about seven or eight years or older. By 1985 exceptions had begun to occur, mainly on the initiative of parents who spontaneously chose to share the consecrated bread with younger children.

It has been accepted that there is no theological reason for excluding younger baptized children from the eucharist. However, practical and pastoral reasons for delaying admission have been advanced. They include:

1. The desire for admission to communion to be a significant and remembered event in the life of the child as it is in the Roman Catholic Church.

2. Admission should follow instruction. Intelligent participation

in the eucharist has a long Anglican history, and New Zealand has produced a very popular teaching resource.

3. From about seven, children are able to conduct themselves with dignity and are able to handle with reverence and care the bread and wine.

4. In the changeover from the practice of admitting teenagers after confirmation, it would have been difficult to win parental acceptance for *infant* communion.

The experience in some other parts of the Anglican Communion suggests that where children are admitted to communion there tends to be a growing demand from parents and children to lower the admission age. This is perhaps encouraged more when there is no formal Admission Service, as in New Zealand. But we are already (in 1985) seeing a readiness to move toward infant communion in some places. This will be encouraged by the Boston recommendations.

## Notes

1. Lambeth Conference 1968, *Resolutions and Reports* (London: SPCK, 1968), Resolution 25, p. 37.

2. The writings of Urban T. Holmes and John Westerhoff have been influential in New Zealand.

3. *Manual of the Constitution, Canons and Standing Orders,* Title G, Canon VIII, p. 240.

4. *Proceedings of the Forty-fourth General Synod* (Church of the Province of New Zealand), Reports, p. 69.

# 9

# New Zealand Initiation Experience: (ii) Acceptance of Child Communion

*Brian Davis and Tom Brown*

### Diocesan and Parish Acceptance

The practice of admitting baptized children to communion before confirmation began "experimentally" in New Zealand in 1970 in the diocese of Waiapu. In 1972, fourteen parishes, all in the diocese of Waiapu, were admitting children to communion prior to confirmation. By 1984, 170 parishes (about half of all parishes in the province) were admitting children to communion. All dioceses were involved, and in one diocese all parishes were committed to the new approach. Today (1991) more than ninety percent of New Zealand parishes practice child communion.

In the diocese of Wellington prior to 1986, the bishop was opposed to the practice and acted to discourage clergy from following the approved provincial guidelines. In 1973, fourteen percent of all Wellington parishes were admitting children to communion prior to confirmation; in 1978 twenty-one percent, in 1983 eighteen percent, and in 1989 sixty-eight percent. These figures underline the significance of the bishop's role in encouraging or frustrating change. The 1983 figure reflects the negative move of the then bishop and the 1989 figure, the fact that his successor was a strong supporter of child communion.

The New Zealand approach of allowing both the traditional and the new practice to continue side by side has been pastorally helpful and avoided general hostility toward the change. Clergy and parishes more open to the new approach have tended to encourage those hesitant to change. Experience of the new way has been positive and, except under episcopal pressure, no parishes having begun to admit children to communion have returned to the traditional pattern or urged child confirmation as an alternative approach to the practice of child communion.

## The Present Situation

*A New Zealand Prayer Book*, which came into use in 1989, offered the province new initiation rites. In 1990 further revised Guidelines for Christian Initiation were approved by General Synod to ensure pastoral consistency with the rubrics of the prayer book. In the introductory section to the baptismal liturgy, the prayer book states:

> When someone is baptized, that person is brought to Jesus Christ, and made a member of Christ's Church.
>
> When a baptism is of a baby or a child the baptized receives the love and shared faith of the family to grow up in Christ.
>
> Through prayer and fellowship within the Body of Christ, God strengthens and nourishes us. (p. 379)

Parents and godparents are exhorted to "encourage their child to take her/his place in the eucharistic community..." (p. 382). The current provincial guidelines, approved in 1990, state:

> The sacramental means of entry and incorporation into the body of Christ occurs through Baptism. The Eucharist is the sacramental means by which members of the Body are sustained and nurtured in that community and is the central act of worship in the Christian Church. Baptism confers full membership of the Church, and therefore provides the ground for admission to Holy Communion. All may therefore

receive communion from the time of their Baptism regardless of age.

Variations in pastoral practice in relation to admission to the communion may be found, but those once admitted (whether at Baptism, or when judged pastorally appropriate by priest and family, or at a special service after more formal instruction, or after receiving the Laying on of Hands for Confirmation), are welcome to receive communion in any parish in the Province.

A process of education is essential in developing an awareness and understanding of the meaning of the Eucharist. Teaching on the Eucharist should be made widely available.

These new guidelines were accepted by the General Synod even though the reference to "instruction approved by the bishop" as a prerequisite for admission remains as a canon. The repeal of this canon is now necessary to remove all legal obstacles to infant communion and give the guidelines unquestionable force.

At this stage the practice of infant communion is exceptional, and most children are being admitted to communion from about the age of seven years, after a period of preparation and special instruction. Teaching resources have been provided within the province, the best known being Graham Brady's *Going to the Supper of the Lord*. A handbook for teachers and a workbook designed for use by children in the seven to ten age group has been particularly popular. More educational resources are currently being prepared.

A constant factor in provincial guidelines has been the requirement of parental approval. Parents are expected to be present with their communicating children. Special adult sponsorship provision is made for baptized children who are admitted but don't have the support of their parents at worship.

## Cultural Factors

The New Zealand approach to reform in the area of Christian initiation, and in particular child communion, allows the main cultural groupings (Maori, Pakeha, and Polynesian), and also the individual dioceses and parishes, to move at their own pace, subject only to the provincial guidelines. Though this has resulted in a diversity of pastoral practice, no serious pastoral confusion or difficulties have arisen. The process of change has been largely problem-free.

The rightness and value of child communion has won overwhelming acceptance among the seven dioceses of the province—what we are now calling "*Tikanga Pakeha*." There has been a slower response to admission of children to communion in both the diocese of Polynesia and *Te Pihopatanga* among Maori Anglicans. *Tikanga Polynesia* and *Tikanga Maori* have been more resistant to ecclesiastical reform generally than has *Tikanga Pakeha*. Cultural rather than theological factors explain this best. No *Tikanga* is opposed to the alternative practice, however, and in time all are likely to follow more fully the lead given by the dominant *Tikanga*.

## Some Challenges

Currently the province is addressing some of the pastoral, educational, and liturgical implications of children at communion. These may be summarized by the following questions:

1. How does a eucharistic community recognize and provide for the presence of children?

2. How does the traditional Sunday School model of Christian nurture need to be modified once children are admitted to communion?

3. What parental or other adult sponsor support does a young child need if he/she is admitted to communion?

4. What teaching and liturgical resources do parishes need to

improve the quality of their ministry to children who are participants in the eucharistic faith community?

## Summary

The movement towards child and infant communion has been welcomed within the Church of the Province of New Zealand. It has required episcopal leadership and the leadership of parish clergy to win the support of the laity. In some places, however, it has been the lay people who have brought pressure to bear for change from the old pattern in the face of reluctant clergy. The province has allowed reform to take place at its own pace, and this has been well accepted. The unevenness of this process of acceptance has not been a pastoral problem.

The benefits of child communion could be identified as follows:

1. The practice recognizes the fullness of baptism as *the* sacrament of membership.

2. The participation of children in eucharistic worship nurtures them in their spiritual growth as members of the body of Christ.

3. The presence of children at the eucharist reminds the local church of the value and importance of children, and of the gifts they bring to the faith community as a whole.

4. The practice of child communion has the effect of transforming aging congregations into family gatherings with all age groups being represented.

5. The practice of child communion has an evangelistic dimension. Children can and do invite their friends to worship, and this can lead to their baptism and/or admission to communion.

# Pushing at the Door: (i) The Church of England

*Donald Gray*

Parochial policies toward children at worship in England have shifted violently in recent years, a shift in emphasis common to all denominations in this country. Neville Clark, the Baptist liturgist, has said that whereas in the past liturgical reconstruction has proceeded without much conscious reference to the child, "today the child can no longer be treated in so cavalier a fashion."[1]

In the Church of England, even as comparatively recently as thirty years ago, it would have been assumed that the Sunday program of any Church of England parish would contain carefully allocated time for the Sunday School. In the majority of parishes these Sunday Schools would meet in the afternoon, although there would be a few which would assemble in the morning and even in the 1950s there would still be places where there were both morning and afternoon Sunday Schools.

A survey conducted in 1955 revealed that 83% of adults over 16 claimed to have attended Sunday School or Bible Class for several years in their childhood (a further 11% had attended for a short time and only 6% never went). The same survey in 1955 also revealed that 54% of English parents claimed their own children were attending Sunday School, whereas the 1989 English Church Census reported that only 14% of children under 15 years of age are in a church-related activity on a typical Sunday. Although the Sunday School is still alive and well in many places, it does not enjoy the benefit of going with a tide of public opinion—the national custom of parentally encouraged child attendance.[2]

## Children in Church

A most significant change in parochial policy came when many parishes realized that children ought not to be isolated from the rest of the worshiping family of the church. The first signs of this change of policy came as more and more parishes fell under the influence of the Parish Communion movement. Families were encouraged to come together to this Parish Communion service (it was often significantly called a Family Communion) with a consequent decline in the emphasis on the traditional form of Sunday School.[3]

In order to integrate children into the worship of the Parish Communion, in some churches the young people assemble with the entire congregation at the beginning of the service but leave the church to receive their own instruction when the sermon is reached and remain in their classes until the end of the service. In other parishes the children are absent only for the period of the sermon, but this method necessitates there being suitable rooms conveniently near, or in, the church. It is a method which usually provokes complaints from teachers that the seven-minute Parish Communion-type sermon gives them no time to develop any worthwhile theme with the children. Another widely adopted method is the one in which the children assemble for their own instruction in their own location and then join the rest of the congregation during the service. The most favored "point of entry" is the Peace. This means that the children can join with the adults for the whole of the eucharistic action having had, as it were, their own ministry of the word in their own classes and at their own level. There is the further advantage in this sequence in that the children are then able to be present for the most visually interesting parts of the eucharist.

## "Blessing" of Children

In the churches in which the children were present during the eucharistic prayer additional participation was thought necessary, and so the children were invited to go up to the rail at the time of communion in order to receive a blessing. The blessing received at the rail, while others are receiving communion, was intended make clear to the children their acceptance in the total life of the Christian family. However, this action, seemingly simple and direct, had the effect of highlighting the confusion about membership and communion!

## Members—or not?

If indeed children are members of the church by their baptism and are fit to approach so near to the altar, why are they then denied the token of their membership? If it is being argued that children would not understand what they are doing in receiving the eucharistic gifts, then we adults are making the most arrogant claims about our own understanding of what can only be described as one of the most profound of all mysteries. Surely we have begun to learn that it is folly to try to simplify the eucharist into the inadequacies of human description.

The Parish Communion was not initially intended to promote the participation of children in the eucharistic worship of the church, but was concerned with bringing the eucharist into the center of the worshiping life of each parish and relating that worship to the total mission of the church to the world.[4] Yet, by encouraging families to come to church together, it has had the effect of highlighting the issue of what level of participation children ought to be offered within the eucharist.

## The Knaresborough Report

A Working Party was asked by a Synod resolution of 1983 to review "the admission of baptized persons to communion before confirmation and experiments that have been undertaken in that field." Their report—*Communion before Confirmation?* (the "Knaresborough Report")[5]—was ready by November 1985. Concluding that "confirmation is not an absolutely necessary prerequisite for the admission of persons to Holy Communion," it made a clear recommendation that baptized children and young persons should be admitted to communion in advance of confirmation. It nevertheless recommended that confirmation should remain in the Church of England "as a sacramental means of grace to accompany an adult profession of faith."[6]

The General Synod, in November 1985, had a "take note" debate in which it had before it the Knaresborough Report and was also allowed to refer to the Boston Statement. By a very large majority the Synod agreed to take note of the report.[7]

Following this debate three dioceses in England were assigned as experimental dioceses for this purpose, and parishes within those dioceses were permitted to take part in the communion before confirmation experiment. The dioceses were contrasting: Manchester (north country, almost entirely urban and industrial), Peterborough (mainly rural, but with many new commuter areas), and Southwark (a mixture of urban deprivation and the Surrey "Gin and Jag" belt).

Then came an impasse: no General Synod debate arranged to take further action on the subject. The House of Bishops sat on it. In answer to a question in 1987 they said that they were waiting for a lead from the Lambeth Conference. After the Conference the excuse was that it was necessary to await diocesan responses to a report of its Board of Education, *Children in the Way.*[8] This report, with its intended *double entendre*, was a plea for the church to take seriously the fact that the world of children has radically changed; that no adult can fully understand what it is like to be a child today and therefore the church needs to look again at its Christian education work. *Inter alia* the report recommended: "A resolution of the issue of Communion before Confirmation is required as a matter of urgency."[9] The report amplified the matter:

They [children] are excluded from the central act of the service. In this sense they are not "members together of the body of Christ." For some parishes this has become a real and urgent pastoral issue, and many diocesan Advisers are conscious of a growing demand for children to be admitted to Communion, or at least for a decision about the issue.[10]

As a result of this, a number of dioceses started attaching motions about children at communion to their responses about *Children in the Way*.

## Reardon Report

Eventually on the morning of 13th July 1991 the General Synod had a wide-ranging debate on the whole issue of Christian initiation based on a report prepared by Canon Martin Reardon.[11] Within that report, Canon Reardon made a personal recommendation that, in addition to the traditional pattern (baptism, confirmation, communion), the church ought to permit either baptism, chrismation and communion of infants, or confirmation at a much earlier age than is at present usual in England. In the afternoon the debate concentrated completely on the Knaresborough report and revealed a wide divergence of views. Whereas in the House of Bishops there was a large majority view that the experiments should be discontinued, in both the House of Clergy and the House of Laity there was a strong contrary feeling, many wishing that the experiment be widened. A composite vote eventually affirmed the traditional sequence of baptism, confirmation, admission to communion as normative in the Church of England; accepted that within this sequence confirmation could take place at an early age; asked the Liturgical Commission to prepare rites for renewal of baptismal vows and for adult commitment; but narrowly refused a request for the preparation of regulations which would enable children to be admitted to holy communion before confirmation.[12]

The result brought widespread disappointment. So it was not surprising that at the next meeting of the Synod (November 1991) the Archbishop of Canterbury was questioned about the situation. He replied:

> The House [of Bishops] agrees to seek appropriate means to monitor and evaluate experiments that are presently taking place and has appointed a small group to consider and to advise on how this might be done...pending the evaluation to which I referred, no further experiments should be agreed.[13]

## Assessment of the Experiment

This process of monitoring was undertaken by Culham College Institute who in 1993 issued a report[14] on 98 of those parishes involved in the experiment. From the information gathered by means of a comprehensive questionnaire, the Institute states that although the verdict is not unanimous, there was a substantial majority, nearly four-fifths of all the parishes which responded to the inquiry and virtually all of those involved fully in the experiment, which is convinced of the positive value of admitting children to communion before confirmation.[15]

## Still Pushing at the Door

There is no sign that the debate will cease. At the time of writing (February 1994) there are three diocesan resolutions on the subject waiting to be debated in the Synod. In the composite resolution of 1991, there was also a request that the House of Bishops prepare a paper in consultation with the Board of Education, the Board of Mission and the Liturgical Commission on patterns of nurture in the faith, including the catechumenate.[16] This working party is expected to report before the end of the year. The report will attempt a rounded approach to the initiation of Christians and therefore will not be able to avoid the issue of communion before confirmation. There is a certain wry humor to be derived from the fact that the Chairman of the Working Party is the Bishop of St. Edmundsbury and Ipswich (John Dennis) who was previously the Bishop of Knaresborough!

Despite the hopes of many bishops (in particular) that this matter will go away, it refuses to do so. The seeming failure of many English bishops to realize that their episcopate will not be diminished if the present-day emphasis on confirmation is in any way diverted is sad. New patterns could not only release time, energy and effort for more broadly based episcopal visitations, but also properly affirm the bishop as *the* minister of initiation.

## Notes

1. Ronald C. D. Jasper, ed., *Worship and the Child: Essays by the Joint Liturgical Group* (London: SPCK, 1975), p. 9.
2. *All God's Children? Children's Evangelism in Crisis*, A report from the General Synod Board of Education and the Board of Mission, GS988, 1991, pp. 3-4.
3. See Donald Gray, *Earth and Altar: The Evolution of the Parish Communion in the Church of England to 1945*, Alcuin Club Collection 68 (Norwich: Canterbury Press, 1986).
4. Ibid., p. 7.
5. *Communion before Confirmation*, Report of the General Synod Board of Education Working Party on Christian Initiation and Participation in the Eucharist, 1985.
6. Ibid., p. 49.
7. General Synod Report of Proceedings, vol. 16, no. 3, pp. 896-929.
8. *Children in the Way: New Directions for the Church's Children*, A report from the General Synod Board of Education.
9. Ibid., p. 91.
10. Ibid., pp. 51-2.
11. *Christian Initiation—A Policy for the Church of England*, A

Discussion Paper by Canon Martin Reardon, GS Misc. 365, 1991.

12. G. S. Report, vol. 22, no. 2, pp. 273-335.

13. Ibid., no. 3, p. 746.

14. Brian Kay, Ian Greenough, John Gay, *Communion Before Confirmation*, A report on the survey conducted by Culham College Institute, Abingdon, Oxford, 1993.

15. Ibid., p. 34.

16. G. S. Report, vol. 22, no. 2, p. 342.

# Pushing at the Door: (ii) The Anglican Church of Australia

*Ronald L. Dowling*

The Australian door needed a second push—in more ways than one! The issue of admitting children to communion first came to General Synod in 1981. That Synod passed a provisional canon which regularized what was already happening in a number of dioceses and one province. A provisional canon required the assent of two-thirds of the Diocesan Synods to come into effect. It failed to get this. Many dioceses found the canon too restrictive or unnecessary. At the August 1985 meeting of General Synod the canon was reintroduced with some proposed amendments. After some of these were accepted and others rejected the final vote was taken. The canon passed both the Houses of Bishops and Laity with the required two-thirds majority, but failed to get the required majority in the House of Clergy by one vote—an abstention! This meant that the canon had failed—to everyone's amazement.

On the next day, the Primate recommitted the vote on advice that a canon should not fail on an abstention. So the door was pushed again and this time the canon passed all Houses (with increased majorities in each house) and was thus adopted by General Synod. Its status is that it comes into operation in each diocese as the Diocesan Synod adopts it. In some dioceses this will mean simply regularizing what is already happening while in others it opens the door for the first time. At the time of writing (1985) less than half the Diocesan Synods have had a chance to consider the matter, and, as far as the writer is aware, it has been adopted by all who have thus far considered it.

Most of the amendments to the previous canon were along the lines of making it clear that baptism is the basis on which children are admitted to communion. This indeed was achieved. However, the admission is to be followed by a subsequent service of confirmation, as the second paragraph of the revised canon shows:

> A child who has been baptized but who has not yet been confirmed, is eligible to be admitted to the Holy Communion if the minister is satisfied that the child has been adequately instructed, gives evidence of appropriate understanding of the nature and meaning of the Holy Communion and has fulfilled the conditions of repentance and faith; and if the child, with the sponsorship of his or her parents or of other confirmed members of the congregation, seeks such admission while awaiting confirmation.

It is the clear intention of the majority of members of General Synod that confirmation must be retained as a rite of personal affirmation and episcopal handlaying and that this rite is mandatory for all who wish to continue in church membership. Attempts to remove all references to confirmation failed.

By the standards and recommendations of the Boston Statement, one would have to say that the Australian church has only opened the door halfway. Although there is no minimum age written into the canon, it is clear that infants and very young children are still precluded from communion. The provisions of "adequate preparation" and "appropriate understanding" and the "conditions of repentance and faith" indicate this. These questions are taken up in Section IIB of the Boston Statement where it asserts the principle that:

> baptism is the sole sacramental qualification for participation in the liturgical and sacramental life of the church...Given this principle, it is paradoxical to

place further hurdles, whether of age, or attainment, or of a sacramental rite of passage, which would have to be reached or crossed before the candidate would begin communicant life, the life of sharing in the *koinonia.*

The Australian church will do well to heed the warnings of Section B, and it is to be hoped that the obstacles inherent in paragraph 2 of the canon will be only interim and not become a permanent feature of the church's initiation practice.

The Boston Statement was issued in the first week of August 1985. The General Synod met during the last week of that month. Although the statement was in the hands of some members, most had not even heard of its existence. This may or may not have been unfortunate. Some commentators are of the opinion that many of the more conservative members would have found the statement to be far too radical. The canon is a conservative one and attempts to move it further forward did not succeed. Perhaps the statement may have frightened off some of these conservatives to the point where no movement would have been possible. On the other hand, many more progressive members still feel that they can, with time, achieve further movement. They are greeting the statement as a real advance and very useful in future deliberations.

The canon that General Synod passed provides for bishops and/or Diocesan Synods to make regulations that will put it into practice. It is too soon yet for any of these regulations to have appeared. For those dioceses which have not been admitting chil dren to communion (there are some where this has been happening for five years or more) the statement will be useful to those who have the responsibility for drawing up any regulations. The statement has been drawn to the church's attention for this purpose. In at least one place it is being used to try to prevent the regulating of any minimum age.

So a door has been opened in Australia. Very soon we should see young baptized children receiving communion in most dioceses.

In those places where it is already happening it has gained wide acceptance. Many families and parishes are rejoicing in their wider eucharistic fellowship, and whole congregations are being nurtured by this. For those who wish to open the door a bit wider there is still much work ahead. The Boston Statement will help the process. Only the future will show how much.

## Addendum (December 1993)

*Ronald L. Dowling*

Since the passing of the Admission to Communion Canon by the Australian General Synod in 1985, all but two of the dioceses (Sydney and The Murray) have adopted the canon. Both Sydney and The Murray hold that the BCP 1662 pattern should be maintained.

In 1991 the Research Officer of the General Synod Office conducted a survey into the practice of baptism, admission of children to communion, and confirmation in this church. The report was published in March 1992. In the section on admission to communion the following features were noted:

1. In nearly all of the dioceses some form of diocesan regulations was in place. Common features included: careful preparation of congregations, parents and the children themselves; that there be some careful program of preparation for the children; that there be some ongoing pattern of education and nurture.

2. In about one-quarter of the dioceses there is no specified minimum age for admission; about half of the dioceses required children to be a minimum age which varied from five to eight years. However, not all dioceses reported on this item.

3. The dioceses were divided about having a special rite of admission. Some required it, some forbade it, and some were noncommittal.

4. The figures showed that in a majority of the dioceses, the vast majority of parishes were participating.

Observation by this writer would seem to indicate that this practice is now widespread across the Australian church and is considered "normal." It would also seem to be the case that in a number of places children are beginning to be admitted at an earlier age. (In my own Diocese of Perth the archbishop has rescinded the minimum age requirement [seven years] and left it to the discretion of the local priest and community.)

It would therefore seem that in the seven or eight years since the General Synod passed the Admission of Children to Communion Canon, the practice has become widely accepted across the Australian church, and that Anglicans in this country accept that baptism is the basis for a person's participation in the eucharist.

# 12

# Ecumenical Perspectives

*Eugene L. Brand*

## 1. Introduction

Is the question of children and the eucharist an ecumenical one? Or better, in what sense is it an ecumenical question? The Lima document, *Baptism, Eucharist and Ministry* (*BEM*), raises it in the Commentary (to B 14 and to E 19):

> Those churches which baptize children but refuse them a share in the eucharist before such a rite [chrismation/confirmation] may wish to ponder whether they have fully appreciated and accepted the consequences of baptism.

> Since the earliest days, baptism has been understood as the sacrament by which believers are incorporated into the body of Christ and are endowed with the Holy Spirit...There is discussion in many churches today about the inclusion of baptized children as communicants at the Lord's Supper.[1]

Such references mark a step forward from the bilateral ecumenical dialogues. In the international bilaterals as well as the national or regional bilaterals known to me, I find no mention of the communion of children as a problem to be addressed. That is even true of the various dialogues with the Orthodox. One cannot say, therefore, that the question of children and the eucharist is a burning issue in the ecumenical debate.

Why is that? In large part, at least, it is due to the ecclesiological gap in the dialogues. We have achieved a degree of convergence on the understanding of the sacraments themselves which is almost miraculous. But the sacraments do not float free in space. They are part of an ecclesiological context and until that context is itself discussed, we cannot be certain whether the sacramental convergence is real or not.

Baptism is a good case in point. Most ecumenists still seem to be of the opinion that baptism is not a major problem. We all agree on what it is, and we all see in it the fundament of and the summons to unity (Ephesians 4.5). The only thing we disagree about—so the common line—is when people who are born into Christian families (or "Christian societies") should be baptized. This line of thought, however, skirts the ecclesiological issue. Though we all agree that baptism births the people of God and that this people is essentially one people, we tend to gloss over the fact that baptism also births a local community in which one lives and experiences the life of the people of God. So long as the local churches were fully in communion, that presented no problem. But since the great schism between East and West, the Reformation of the sixteenth century, the rise of denominationalism in Britain, and the modern proliferation of separated Christian communities, it constitutes a serious problem: that of mutual recognition of baptism. It is with this ecclesiological issue that "the rubber hits the road," for mutual recognition cannot simply be taken for granted, not even among those churches who have already agreed on their understanding of the sacrament itself.[2] We have yet to face squarely the question of whether membership in the local (denominational or confessional) church really is understood to be simultaneous with membership in the Church Catholic. Perhaps we have been only wishing it were so.

Having made that observation, I can now go on to say that the question of children and the eucharist is on the ecumenical agenda—just as it is on the internal agenda of individual Christian communions—whether that is currently recognized or not. Especially is it true, of course, for those churches who baptize infants but do not immediately admit them to the fellowship of the altar. The question is on the agenda because our affirmations about baptism and the eucharist have put it there, and it is to the credit of *BEM* that it takes note of that.

## 2. The Emergence of the Question

As a contemporary question, the communion of children seems to have arisen among those concerned pastorally about liturgy. Once raised, the issue has stimulated research into the liturgical and ecclesiological traditions. But it is important to keep in mind that the communion of children is raised as a pastoral, not an academic, issue. And, one must hasten to add, the laity may well have recognized the issue before it came to the attention of the clergy.

There are at least three factors which have brought the matter to the fore. The first has to do with the rediscovery of the eucharist as corporate meal by those whose eucharistic piety and practice was previously largely individualistic, "consumer" oriented. Where the eucharist has regained its place as the chief Sunday service and where it is understood as the shared meal offered the community by its Lord, the problem of excluding the children becomes increasingly acute. If children have been baptized and thus become members of the community, what are the grounds for excluding them?

A second factor is society's changed perception of children and of their role in any community. The report of a World Council of Churches consultation on the communion of children points to a new body of knowledge in psychology and education explaining how and what children learn at various stages in their development. The report also notes the change in the societal position of children. In many places they have "been freed from the traditional patterns of authority which kept them subservient" to adults and have been recognized as "persons with particular gifts, needs and abilities."[3] We are warned not to think that "children can understand only what they can express," and that the judgment "they are too young to understand" too easily becomes a self-fulfilling prophecy.[4] Regarding "meaningful participation in the eucharist," Elaine Ramshaw has observed:

> I have not yet seen anyone suggest that one way of finding out whether participation is meaningful to children is to observe whether or not non-participation is meaningful to them. I have seen no one discuss the psychological effects of exclusion on children, though I have heard numerous personal accounts of people who observed in children (or experienced in their own childhood) the pain of being left out...psychological research could tell us a good deal about what inclusion or exclusion means to the child, if we care to find out.[5]

I confess to being one who opposes adjusting ecclesial practice to suit prevailing insights in education and/or psychology. At the same time, however, a pastoral orientation requires the best insight available into those people placed in one's charge.

A third factor is our rediscovery of eschatology, not so much as the doctrine of the last things, but rather as the hermeneutical key to almost everything. When the community of the faithful is understood as participating already in that future toward which God is leading, so that the community becomes itself a sign of that future, then questions of membership and faith take on new perspectives.

Historical research prompted by the question of children's communion has demonstrated what could be a possible fourth factor: even in the "Western" church, the communion of all the baptized (including infants) was the prevailing practice into the High Middle Ages and in some places may have continued even longer.[6] Factors leading to its demise were different from arguments now raised against it. The burden of proof, it would seem, is on those who resist following the tradition of more than one millennium in the West and almost two in the East.

## 3. Ecclesiological Assumptions

This paper operates with two ecclesiological assumptions: (1) there is only one category of membership in the Church Catholic: baptized membership; (2) the body of Christ (eucharist) is for the body of Christ (Church). Where these assumptions are shared, one can answer the question of children and the eucharist theologically (=ecclesiologically) only one way: there is no reason for excluding any member of the church, regardless of age, from the eucharist unless they have blocked their own way to the Lord's Table by becoming subject to discipline or by lapsing.

My first assumption is reflected in a sampling of ecumenical documentation. From *Baptism, Eucharist and Ministry* (B 6): "Through baptism, Christians are brought into union with Christ, with each other and with the Church of every time and place." From the Anglican-Lutheran dialogue: "The baptized are grafted into the Church..."[7] From the Anglican-Orthodox dialogue: "The Church is 'the body of Christ'...The head is Christ..., and his members are those who in faith respond to the gospel..., are baptized in the name of the Father, the Son, and the Holy Spirit..., and are united with Christ and with each other through participation in the Eucharist..."; "We are agreed in regarding the Church as a eucharistic community..."[8]

The Anglican-Orthodox citation is a bridge to documentation reflecting my second assumption. From the Anglican/Roman Catholic *Final Report*:

> In guarding and developing communion, every member has a part to play. Baptism gives everyone in the Church the right, and consequently the ability, to carry out his particular function in the body. The recognition of this fundamental right is of great importance...[9]

Even though this statement is about "The Place of the Laity" in regard to Venice's "Authority in the Church," surely its basic application would have to be participation in the Eucharist!

This sampling indicates that my two assumptions are by no means idiosyncratic; they are part of the ecumenical convergence. But one looks in vain for a discussion of the central question of this paper. If that lack could be attributed to the general omission of dealing with ecclesiological questions, one could be somewhat reassured, the more so since the question of what, in practice, constitutes membership is seldom discussed. What one does find here and there is a reiteration of traditional "Western" positions showing that the confusion regarding Christian initiation remains unclarified and revealing a failure to draw obvious ecclesiological conclusions from stated premises of sacramental theology.

Only two Christian communions are really consistent in practice with the current theology of baptism and church membership: the Orthodox and the non-pedobaptist churches (i.e., churches which practice "believer's" baptism) of the "West." Both celebrate the rites of Christian initiation in uninterrupted sequence so that no differentiation between baptized members and communicant members is possible.

## 4. The "Western" Question

The communion of children, then, is a question raised for the pedobaptist churches of the "West" by the premises of their own sacramental theology. Not only have these communions— Anglican, Lutheran, Methodist, Reformed, Roman Catholic— continued the practice of separating temporally components of Christian initiation, with one exception their practice has been shaped by being established and/or folk churches. That means they have practiced infant baptism indiscriminately, at least according to contemporary standards of judgment. And though they have differed in their understanding of its nature and its proper minis-

ter, they have thought of confirmation as the necessary complement to infant baptism.

A survey prepared for the 1980 World Council of Churches
consultation on communion with children documents the trend of
lowering the age for the "first communion" of those baptized as
infants. The trend is clear, though conditions for admission vary
and the relationship between first communion and confirmation is
solved in various ways. Included are the Roman Catholic Church,
Lutheran churches (Denmark, Finland, Norway, North America,
Germany), the Anglican Communion, Presbyterian churches
(United States, New Zealand, Scotland), the Methodist Church in
England, and the Reformed Church in Switzerland.[10]

One can only rejoice at such developments and in the knowledge that they are spreading. But none of them strikes at the heart
of the "Western" problem regarding infant baptism as complete
initiation. They are predicated on the need for instruction preced-
ing first communion. Often all that has changed is the concept of
educational psychology: the child is capable of the requisite understanding at an earlier age than was previously thought. Theological
and ecclesiological perceptions remain untouched. A pointed
example is provided by the German Lutheran churches.

A document of the German Lutheran-Roman Catholic dialogue
includes a forthright statement about church fellowship being
founded in baptism and lived out in participation in the eucharist.
Yet in the same document the Lutherans evaluate positively the
separation of confirmation (and thus first communion) from
infant baptism on pastoral grounds. Fundamentally, they say, the
baptized infant is entitled to the eucharist, but they insist that pastoral responsibility requires that the "concrete admission to communion" be connected with confirmation since it implies having
come to a basic understanding of Christian faith. Even though
children are in fact being admitted to the Lord's Table before confirmation, a note makes clear that the principle that confirmation
constitutes admission to holy communion still stands in German

Lutheran churches.[11] This is but one example of the uneasiness about infant baptism in the West.

I suggest that the uneasiness with seeing in infant baptism complete initiation has two roots. One is the legitimate need to connect a concept of sacramental efficacy with a response of faith. The other is that when infant baptism is practiced indiscriminately, the insistence upon instruction and understanding tends to weed out the hangers-on. That would seem to be corroborated by a different movement in some folk churches to abolish infant baptism altogether, also to weed out the hangers-on.

One can also rejoice that lowering the age of first communion has often broken the link with confirmation so that at least no ritual impediment blocks the path from the font to the altar. That constitutes progress by removing one more argument for a confirmation separated from baptism.

Being positive about communicating children at an earlier age cannot substitute for addressing the ecclesiological problem in the pedobaptist communions of the West. To do that requires dealing with the communion of infants.

## 5. The Communion of Infants

If the pedobaptist churches of the "West" are to restore the communion of infants, they must do it in a "Western" manner. To advocate or to defend infant communion is not necessarily to attempt an "Orthodox-izing" of "Western" Christianity. What is needed is a way of understanding sacramental efficacy that deals adequately with the response of faith. For "Western" churches will not be content with a sacramental theology which seems mechanistic, one in which the response of faith has no necessary place.

One solution is suggested by those who advocate enrolling infants in the catechumenate, thereby "attaching" them to the community of faith. The catechumenate would culminate in the rites of initiation celebrated in unbroken sequence and at an age when they can be consciously experienced and understood. It is a solution which parallels the practice of the non-pedobaptist churches, while not adopting their sacramental theology. Actually, however, it attempts to solve the problem of the pedobaptist churches by eliminating it. If the earlier pressure to baptize infants as soon as possible to save them from damnation should they die unexpectedly is no longer felt, then it is difficult to condemn this solution out of hand.

Where there is a strong sense of local community and of the sacraments as constituting and strengthening that community, however, the decision of the early church to baptize infants born into its circle and to welcome them at the Lord's Table still seems the natural and desirable course of action. No indiscriminate communicating of indiscriminately baptized infants! Infant communion and carefully delimiting the scope of infant baptism must go together. But where they do, a natural and appropriately variegated sense of Christian community results.

The need for a disciplined approach to the initiation of infants is part of taking the "Western" heritage seriously. Another part is the question of faith.[12]

As classically stated, Lutheran sacramental theology is as objective as anyone could wish for. The sacraments, rightly administered, are effective because their efficacy depends upon God, not upon our faith. Central to the classical Lutheran concept is the possibility of the *manducatio impiorum*. But it is there overall in the gift-character of the sacraments too. Nevertheless it was impossible to speak of sacraments and thus of infant baptism without speaking of faith. As I have noted elsewhere, the Lutheran fathers, in defending the necessity (à la Augustine) of infant baptism, did it not only on the basis of grace but also on the basis of faith. They simply posited infant faith, equating it with the operation of the Holy Spirit in baptism. "This action or operation of the Holy Spirit in infants we call faith, and say that infants believe."[13] Such an argument is problematical today but its intention was correct, and the theological necessity of it was quintessentially "Western."

Here is where an eschatological perspective can assist us. I would argue that we may baptize infants unto faith who are born into the community of faith, that precisely because of our trust in God's promised future for his people and the action of the Holy Spirit among us, we can trust that given the environment of the fellowship of the church and of a Christian home, faith will grow and mature. If such a conviction allows us to baptize, it also allows us to complete the process of initiation with first communion. Frank Senn has written approvingly,

> This view emphasizes not just the character of faith as a gift of the Holy Spirit, but also the eschatological nature of the Church. One is baptized into the community of promise and is nurtured in that promise of forgiveness and reconciliation by Holy Communion.[14]

So long as we see the community of faith and the faith of its members in eschatological perspective, it is completely illogical to baptize infants and then withhold from them the nourishment for the pilgrimage into which they have been enrolled. The proclamation of the Gospel is absolutely crucial in this baptism unto faith, and our talk of sacramental efficacy must not ignore that.

This eschatological view of things is harmonious with the ecumenical document, *Baptism, Eucharist and Ministry*:

> B 7: [Baptism] gives participation in the community of the Holy Spirit. It is a sign of the Kingdom of God and of the life of the world to come.

> B 8: Baptism is both God's gift and our human response to that gift. It looks towards a growth into the measure of the stature of the fullness of Christ. The necessity of faith for the reception of the salvation embodied and set forth in baptism is acknowledged by all churches.

> B 9: Baptism is related not only to momentary experience, but to lifelong growth into Christ...In this new relationship, the baptized live for the sake of Christ, of his Church and of the world which he

loves, while they wait in hope for the manifestation of God's new creation and for the time when God will be all in all...

E 26: As it is entirely the gift of God, the Eucharist brings into the present age a new reality which transforms Christians into the image of Christ and therefore makes them his effective witnesses...The eucharistic community is nourished and strengthened for confessing by word and action the Lord Jesus Christ who gave his life for the salvation of the world...

Perhaps the clearest expression of the eschatological perspective is in the 1984 report of the Anglican-Reformed International Commission:

In our water-baptism we are brought sacramentally into union with the once-for-all Baptism of Jesus on behalf of all mankind... As the baptism of Jesus was a beginning, prophetically embracing both its fulfillment in his ministry and its consummation in his death and resurrection, so the baptism of a Christian is likewise the beginning of a process... This Christ, the one for many, baptizes the Church by the Spirit, that as one body we may participate with him in his ministry of reconciliation, to restore to all nations their true humanity as the children of one father...[15]

From this clear eschatological stance, one could have gone on to draw the conclusions we have suggested for baptism and faith which would make possible the complete initiation of infants in churches with a "Western" pedobaptist heritage.

Let me inject a final observation. When dealing with the response of faith, it is all too easy to slip into the fallacy of categories, forgetting that it is individual persons we baptize and nourish with word and eucharist. Why must the response of faith which baptism entails be a public personal profession or a participation in the sacrament of penance? The categorical statement of the Anglican-Lutheran document, "The practice of infant baptism necessitates the provision of opportunity for personal profession of faith before the congregation" (i.e., confirmation), seems guilty of that fallacy.[16] Surely participation in the eucharist is itself a personal response of faith, as is diaconal service. Public affirmation of one's baptism may also be the appropriate response, but why only once in life? The eschatological perspective would call for participation in the life and ministry of the pilgrim people and see that as evidence of faith. And such participation can only be that appropriate to the age and situation of the person in question.

## 6. The Ecumenical Significance of the Question

In the final section of this paper I must, in summary fashion, point to what is at stake ecumenically in dealing with the question of the communion of children and especially of infants.

First, admitting all baptized persons to the fellowship of the eucharist provides the solution to the ecclesiological problem of church membership. So long as pedobaptist churches withhold communion from infants and young children we are faced with theologically impossible alternatives: either an unbiblical differentiation among members of the body of Christ or a platonic concept of that body into which non-communicating infants are said to have been incorporated.

Second, upholding and preserving the sacramental understanding of Christian initiation is especially crucial in the ecumenical mix. Among Baptists there is a growing hesitancy to describe baptism as an ordinance or sign for fear of emptying the rich meaning of baptism which New Testament studies have revealed.[17] As many Baptists search for a "middle position," it is important that the sacramental understanding held by the pedobaptists not be discredited by an inability to solve adequately the problem of church membership.

Third, the implementation and reception of bilateral dialogue agreements will require clarity on this question. In Anglican-Lutheran relationships, for example, if the "Cold Ash Report" (1983) recommendation is implemented that "interim eucharistic sharing" be explored in areas beyond the United States with the goal being full communion,[18] then it would be important to work together toward an answer to the question of the communion of infants and young children. In the meantime there is the practical problem in any service where the eucharist is shared by two communions, if the question of children's communion is not similarly answered. It is not helpful if one communion is, as it were, blackmailed by the practice of the other.

Fourth, an omission needs to be explained. In raising the issue of infant communion and thus, the reintegration of Christian initiation for infants, I have not used relationships with the Orthodox churches as an argument. That is because, strictly speaking, it is not possible for the Orthodox to recognize the validity of sacraments celebrated outside their own churches. The ecumenical issues of ecclesiology between "East" and "West" are, therefore, more fundamental than the question we are dealing with.[19]

Fifth, but pastorally first, the proper answer to the question of the communion of children is crucial to their own spiritual formation as individuals, their understanding of and faithful participation in the church's worship, and their grasp of the corporate character of the church. But that is only the beginning. It is also crucial to the development of a full and natural spirituality in the families of the church and to the success of the catechetical efforts of the parents. And finally it is crucial to the health of the local community, keeping it liturgically and spiritually flexible and preserving it from an arid intellectualism. Acting on the fact that baptized children are full members of the community could bring alive many a dull and dreary congregation!

# Notes

1. *Baptism, Eucharist and Ministry*, Faith and Order Paper 111 (Geneva: World Council of Churches, 1982). Citations of this document will be according to section and paragraph, e.g., B 14 = Baptism section, paragraph 14.

2. The issue is too complex to develop here. See my paper for Societas Liturgica, 1985, "The Lima Text as a Standard for Current Understandings and Practice of Baptism," section 3, in *Studia Liturgica* 16 (1986):40-63; and note 19 below.

3. G. Müller-Fahrenholz, ed., *...and do not hinder them*, Faith and Order Paper 109 (Geneva: World Council of Churches, 1982), pp. 6-7.

4. Elaine Ramshaw, "Sacramental Readiness and Psychology," *Liturgy* 1 (1981):47.

5. Ibid., p. 49.

6. Documentation in J. D. C. Fisher, *Christian Initiation: Baptism in the Medieval West* (London: SPCK, 1965); cf. David R. Holeton, "The Communion of Infants and Young Children," Faith and Order Paper 109, pp. 59-69.

7. Pullach Report (1972), in H. Meyer and L. Vischer, eds., *Growth in Agreement*, Faith and Order Paper 108 (Ramsey, NJ: Paulist Press, 1984), p. 22. This position was reaffirmed by the European Regional Commission in its Helsinki Report, 1982 (London: SPCK, 1983), p. 10.

8. Dublin Agreed Statement (London: SPCK, 1984), pp. 9-10, 47.

9. Faith and Order Paper 108, p. 102.

10. Faith and Order Paper 109, pp. 70-81. A Lutheran example: In 1978 children at Grade 5 or below were admitted to Holy Communion in 48% of the congregations of the Lutheran Church in America. By 1983 it had risen to 63.1% (1983 LCA Congregational Report).

11. *Kirchengemeinschaft in Wort und Sakrament* (Paderborn/Hanover: Verlag Bonifacius und Lutherisches

Verlagshaus, 1984), pp. 32, 34 and note 19, p. 103. Unless one can point to actual activities and privileges into which baptism initiates, the statement about fundamental entitlement remains remarkably platonic. See also *Report of the Studies on Confirmation*...(Geneva: LWF Department of Studies, 1983).

12. A Lutheran may be expected to add yet another part related to the ability to examine oneself and thus avoid unworthy reception (1 Corinthians 11.27ff). Though that has been a factor in the position of pedobaptist churches, my perception is that it no longer is. I have omitted considering it primarily because it seems insignificant in the ecumenical discussion. But see K. H. Bieritz, "The Lord's Supper As Sacrament of Fellowship," Faith and Order Paper 109, pp. 38-50.

13. See my "Baptism and Communion of Infants: A Lutheran View," *Worship* 50 (1976): 33ff.

14. "Issues in Infant Communion," *Dialog* 22 (1983):222.

15. *God's Reign and Our Unity* (London: SPCK, 1984), par. 51, 56, 60.

16. Pullach Report (1972), par. 66, Faith and Order Paper 108, p. 22.

17. See "Baptists and Ecumenicity with Special Reference to Baptism," Faith and Order Paper 97, in *Review and Expositor* 77 (1980): 35-36.

18. *Report of the Anglican-Lutheran Joint Working Group* (London/Geneva: Anglican Consultative Council and Lutheran World Federation, 1983), p. 16.

19. See *Mutual Recognition of Baptism in Interchurch Agreements*, Faith and Order Paper 90 (Geneva: World Council of Churches, 1978), p. 20.

# Children and Communion

*An International Anglican Liturgical Consultation Held in Boston*
U.S.A. 29-31 July 1985

## I. Introduction: An Overview of the Provinces

At the 1968 Lambeth Conference the Provinces of the Communion were asked to examine the theology of initiation and admission to communion. This has been done in some Provinces[1] and not in others. In those Provinces where work has been undertaken there has been a variety of theological stances and practices. In most of these Provinces change has taken place or is in process. In many places children are being admitted to communion at their baptism or at a time well before the traditional age of confirmation and first communion.

Some Provinces have formally changed their practice. It is in accordance with the American Book of Common Prayer (1979) and the Canadian *Book of Alternative Services* (1985) that the newly baptized should receive communion at their baptism (regardless of age) and remain communicants thereafter. In New Zealand the "alternative practice" of beginning to receive communion around seven or eight has become a general practice since it was introduced in the 1970s. In Scotland permission has been given to admit the unconfirmed to communion as it has in some dioceses in Central Africa and on a local basis in Southern Africa.

Other Provinces are in the process of changing their practice. England has been studying the possibility of change since the publication of the Ely Report in 1971. A number of diocesan bishops have permitted and encouraged the admission of young children to the eucharist, a practice recommended to the General Synod by the Knaresborough Report of 1985. In Australia a 1981 "provisional canon" to permit unconfirmed children to receive communion did not receive the required approval of diocesan synods. A number of dioceses, however, admit children to communion before confirmation. The question is being raised again at the 1985 General Synod.

Some Provinces, like Ireland and Wales, are in the process of studying the question but have not taken any measure which would admit the unconfirmed to communion.

Finally, it appears that many Provinces have not seriously discussed the question at all.

Out of this a variety of developments have taken place which elicit a number of questions or observations.

## A. Theological Issues

Although there is a high degree of theological agreement among those Provinces which have issued new theological statements on initiation, it is not yet apparent that there is a common theology of initiation throughout the Anglican Communion.[2] This applies particularly to the theology and practice of confirmation. Although new theological reports have emphasized the unity of the initiation rite, urging that the baptized should be admitted to the eucharist,[3] in fact a separate rite of confirmation continues to exist which, in many Provinces, is still the usual rite of admission to communion.

## B. Cultural Considerations

Many Provinces which have not tackled the issue have had more pressing issues to face during this period, such as civil war or religious persecution. ACC-6 has asked that the question of the admission of children to communion continue to be pressed.[4] We therefore believe that the following questions should be faced:

(i) What is the place given to children in a particular society?

(In some cultures children are encouraged to make their desires known, whereas in others there is no question of this. In some cultures children regularly eat with adults while in others they always eat separately.)

(ii) Has admission to communion come to be associated with traditional rites of passage and/or adulthood?

(This may have resulted from methods of evangelization in the past in which rites of adulthood became the time for confirmation and therefore admission to communion.)

(iii) Has confirmation come to be used as a means of ensuring that candidates have sufficient knowledge?

(This may particularly be the case where the church wishes to distinguish clearly between Christian and non-Christian cultural elements.)

These issues obscure the theological consequences of baptism. Have they led us to treat baptized Anglican children as if they were only catechumens? We seriously question whether or not these cultural factors can continue to be used to exclude children from the eucharist.

## C. Pastoral and Educational Considerations

It is true that change can involve some pain, and a time of transition is hard for those who liked things as they were, and also for those who want it all to happen everywhere immediately. But difficulties in transition ought not to deter our Anglican Provinces from making sensitive changes if they are right in themselves. We believe that this one deserves urgent consideration.

## II. Theological Dimensions of the Question
### A. Ecclesiological

The various national or regional churches which together comprise the "Anglican" fellowship are often referred to as the "Anglican

Communion." The term "communion" is not used as an evasion of the word "church," but rather as an image of what the true nature of the church is understood to be. The church is the whole body of the faithful. It is created through baptism into the death and resurrection of Jesus Christ, which is the sign of faith and of participation in God's act of redemption.

The faithful sustain and proclaim their unity with their Lord and each other as they meet each Lord's Day and as they regularly participate in the eucharistic assembly by sharing in the Word of God, the prayers, the kiss of peace and the eucharistic gifts. In this way a sharing community, or *koinonia*, is formed and nurtured.

The people of God together form a communion. The shared identity first established in baptism is exhibited and reinforced in communion. Although the biblical evidence which underlies this assertion is not abundant, yet the ecclesiological connection between baptism and the eucharist is well-attested. Thus, to cite but a few instances, on the day of Pentecost the newly baptized were incorporated immediately into the communal meals (Acts 2.41-47); the Corinthians were told that all have been baptized into Christ and shared the sacred meal, and that these factors, shared by all, are the background to the judgment of God upon some (1 Cor. 10.2-6). Later, in the same letter, the Corinthians are told that the eucharist is the means of being constituted as the body of Christ (1 Cor. 10.17), a result which, in a later chapter, is said to stem from being baptized (1 Cor. 12.13). The baptized life in Christ is a eucharistic life. The *koinonia* of God's people is a *koinonia* of the baptized.

Although baptism occurs once in the pilgrimage of an individual, whereas the eucharist is a recurrent experience, both complement each other, each pointing to our union with Christ in his death and resurrection, each pointing to our common life in the Spirit, each pointing to our mutual engagement in the bonds of love in the Christian *koinonia*. The maturing of Christian life of both the congregation and the individuals within it may be understood as the unfolding in the common life of the body of Christ of the implications of the one baptism.

## B. Children in Church

We are members of a great Communion in which infants have traditionally been eligible for baptism. The theological arguments for this are lengthy, and the ground has shifted somewhat with the disappearance of "Christendom" and the emergence of a missionary calling for a church which is set in a secular or at least unsympathetic society. Determination as to which infants should be accepted for baptism has also become sensitive in the transition to a post-Christian context. Both issues require further discussion, but here we take as evident the biblical warrant for the baptism of at least some infants, and confine our discussion to a reflection on the role and needs of those infants who are in fact baptized.

Consideration of the arguments for the baptism of infants, insofar as they are ecclesiological arguments, suggests that the communion of such infants should take place from the time of, and on the basis of, their baptism. Baptism is one (Eph. 4.4); if infants are baptized, they are baptized into Jesus Christ just as adults are, and their baptism is in principle initiation into the eucharistic life just as is the baptism of an adult. To postpone their participatory inclusion into the eucharistic community obscures the meaning of their baptism, and even creates a separate and indefensible category of "infant" baptism which has a different initiatory force from that of "adult" baptism. This implies a division in the given unity of our understanding of baptism as incorporation into Christ.

Despite the inherited pattern of Anglicanism, namely, infant baptism followed after a lapse of several years by confirmation and admission to communion, the true difficulty lies not in spelling out the initiatory force of baptism which admits to communion, but in finding any justification for continuing now the inherited pattern of the sixteenth century. Although the relationship of faith to baptism may need further exposition, yet the assertion of the principle that baptism is the sole sacramental qualification for participation in the liturgical and sacramental life of the church is generally accepted.

Given this principle, it is paradoxical to admit children to membership in the body of Christ through baptism, and yet to deny that membership in the eucharistic meal that follows. Given this principle, it is paradoxical to assert that communion is a "means of grace" and yet to insist that children must show "signs of grace" before they be given the eucharistic "means of grace." Given this principle, it is paradoxical to place further hurdles, whether of age, or of attainment, or of a sacramental rite of passage, which would have to be reached or crossed before the candidate could begin communicant life, the life of sharing in the *koinonia*. Yet all these anomalies have been widely practiced by Anglicans.

Before questions are raised with regard to educational or psychological models, we wish to affirm on theological grounds that children of all ages are included among those for whom Christ died, that children of all ages are recipients of his love, that children of all ages are equally persons in the people of God, and that children of all ages have an active ministry in Christ among his people and in the world. We see no dogmatic or other credible basis for regarding some who are baptized as eligible to receive communion while others are not. We believe this is to run contrary to the inclusive character of the Gospel set out in Galatians 3.27-29.

The baptized of all ages are to be treated by the church as believers unless they apostasize or depart into unbelief. The chronological measurement of their life on this earth is of little relevance to that principle. In recent pastoral practice, the baptismal liturgy has itself been celebrated normatively in the context of the eucharist, producing the strange result that the infant or child who has been the focus during the administration of baptism is thereafter set aside from the action and is excluded from sharing in the eucharistic meal. Anglicans need to reflect carefully on this peculiar phenomenon and to ask themselves what it is saying to the wider community about our understanding of the connection between baptism and eucharist which such a practice reveals.

## C. Thresholds Other than Baptism?

Anglicanism has maintained two different quasi-initiatory thresholds for candidates to cross if they are to be welcome at communion. Both have some historical rationale, but on closer inspection distort the meaning of Christian initiation with regard both to baptism and the eucharist. Further, they distort our understanding of the grace of God.

### 1.

The first such threshold is confirmation. Although Cranmer kept the outline of Western medieval confirmation, he shifted the emphasis from the administration of the outward rite to the catechizing which preceded it. Thus, in different ways, the emphasis lay upon the instruction and the necessity of having reached the required age to receive it, rather than upon the sacramental meaning or initiatory force of the laying on of hands itself. Administration of confirmation was lax, or even neglected altogether, for three centuries after the Reformation. It was only with the advent of the strict churchmanship of the nineteenth century that regular pastoral provision for confirmation became normal. This development brought in its train a sacramental view of confirmation different from anything which had had wide currency before.

This doctrinal position was based upon a very literal understanding of the confirmation rubric which made confirmation the prerequisite to receiving communion. There thus emerged the view that without the rite of confirmation, neither non-Anglicans nor unconfirmed children might be admitted to communion. Theology developed beyond the discipline itself and set out the view, popularly known as the "Mason-Dix" line, that confirmation is the second and completing half of the full sacrament of initiation. This school of thought had a dominant influence in the Anglican Communion from about 1890 until 1970. It affected our ecumenical relationships, our liturgical revision, our age of confirmation and also what bishops preached at services of confirmation. It was expressed by several prominent scholars in various ways, but it has now waned because its theological self-confidence has been undermined by further reflection upon the nature of baptism, upon the origins of the baptismal liturgy in the early centuries, and upon its relation to the eucharistic context. The foundation upon which the "Mason-Dix" approach was ostensibly based, historical inquiry, proved to be its weakest dimension.

We do not now believe that inherited understandings of confirmation ought to provide a barrier to the admission of baptized children to communion. Entry upon the communicant life must be detached from confirmation or any variant on it, and should be directly related to baptismal initiation. Any additional ceremonies which Provinces may use in baptism, such as signing with the cross, anointing with oil, or giving of a candle, should not be seen as essential parts of the rite. Thus such ceremonies need not be supplied to complete sacramental initiation nor do they correspond to what has been traditionally called confirmation by Anglicans.

## 2.

The other threshold which is often required is that of a minimum age, which the Reformers concealed within confirmation. It is now encouraged as a next stage when the confirmation threshold is discarded. Children are expected to reach a certain age, to articulate a simple understanding, or even to receive a modest preparation prior to receiving the eucharistic gifts. In other approaches, they must demonstrate a standard of behavior or of spiritual insight. Although not all of these requirements are immediately evident as demanding a minimum age, they come down to that in the end.

We recognize the practical need which Anglicans in some societies may feel for a halfway stage, but we fear that such a halfway point may become a fixed pastoral solution. Liturgical interrogation and celebration accompanying admission to communion at an age of, say, nine or seven or five, may tend to institutionalize the "minimum age" threshold. Our judgment is that it still does not take baptism sufficiently seriously as incorporation into the eucharistic life. Nor does it take seriously the way in which the whole church, by celebrating baptism and eucharist and by practicing everything else which builds up the community, proclaims the meaning of its baptismal life and affirms its being as a community of Christian faith which transcends boundaries of understanding, differences of temperament and varieties of gifts within the one body.[5]

## D. Further Implications

We note briefly some further implications:

(i)  The above discussion leaves open whether some role for a non-initiatory pastoral rite of confirmation, perhaps preceded by a period of preparatory instruction, should be found. It is likely that there will remain a place for a solemn rite of renewal of baptismal vows, perhaps spelling out the implications of baptism for discipleship and the exercise of responsibility in the church. Such a rite, while including the laying on of hands, would have no bearing on admission to the eucharist.

(ii)  Nor does the above discussion raise the question of the role of the bishop in a renewed pattern of initiation. We would neither prescribe nor inhibit an episcopal role. We simply believe that the church must first get its initiation principles right, and then seek ways in which the ordained ministry, through presiding and participation, may be appropriately integrated in the rites. We do, however, favor an increased frequency in the occasions when the bishop will preside at baptismal eucharists.

(iii)  Baptism is initiation into the mission and the ministry of the church, and the liturgy of baptism expresses this. If children are then excluded from the eucharist, it is likely that their exclusion will touch their mission and ministry also. Similarly, their full inclusion in the eucharist should draw out their role in the mission and ministry of the whole people of God.

## E. Some Contextual Considerations

The Anglican Communion has Provinces in which traditional Christian culture is still a strong factor in the life of a society; it has Provinces in which such traditions were once strong, but are now on the decline; it has Provinces in which over the last one to two hundred years forceful missionary work has led to the establishment of churches that are strong, and often growing, and which play a significant, though not necessarily dominant, role in society. It also has Provinces in which Christianity has always been, and continues to be, a minority religion, sometimes of infinitesimal size.

These factors affect the nature and vitality of local eucharistic communities, and they also affect the attitudes of people to new ideas about children receiving communion before confirmation, whether at a very early age, or at a specially fixed age. For example, there are dioceses in England and parts of North America and Australia in which folk religion exerts a strong influence on local life; this may result in hostility to what is seen to be a drastic change in the ordering of society, or alternatively such a new development may actually be welcomed as a legitimate growth from an old pattern to a new one. On the other hand, there are dioceses in various parts of the world in which the so-called collapse of Christendom has produced scattered eucharistic communities which are vigorous in character, and in which the delineation between who is Christian and who is not is strongly felt.

Other churches of the Western tradition are undergoing similar changes of structure and life. There are indications among Roman Catholics, Lutherans, Methodists and Presbyterians of a comparable response to these pressures, but with the obvious difference among most of them that there is no traditional association of confirmation with the bishop as an exclusive role. (Roman Catholic extension of presbyteral confirmation is changing the scene yet further.) It is important that ecumenical dialogue with these churches include discussion about the policy and practice of admission of young children to communion, as well as the way in which liturgical practice is affected by this development.

It is our considered opinion that the phenomenon of children receiving communion at an early age will grow irresistibly in the Anglican Communion, as well as in the other churches just mentioned. As society changes, and as Christian values come to be seen to be held firmly by a minority within an increasingly alien society (rather than loosely held by historic structures within the society), such a development can only serve to strengthen the witness of Christianity as a whole. Worship is our public and corporate profession of faith, where we come together to celebrate the word and sacraments, so that we ourselves may be caught up continually in that eternal proclamation of the wonders of him who has called us out of darkness into his own marvelous light (1 Peter 2.9).

## III. Pastoral Issues

As the first section of this report documents the diversity of practice in the Anglican Communion we intend in this section to set out as best we can the pastoral practice that we believe follows from the principles outlined above. So, for example, we deliberately adopt the full consequence of our theological conviction that infant communion should follow infant baptism, although we recognize that in some places regular communion may be somewhat delayed and that in some Provinces the fixing of a minimum age has helped them to come to terms with this shift in Anglican practice. Whatever pattern prevails, and whatever local variations exist, it is imperative that those admitted to communion are accepted as communicants wherever they worship in the Anglican Communion.

### The Suggested Pattern

We set out here the pattern we should like to see for children with at least one baptized and believing parent, although we recognize that a wide variety of marital, household and cultural patterns exist.

 (i) Members of the congregation should be involved in the preparation of parents for the baptism of their children.

 (ii) Parents should be the chief sponsors for their children and may be joined by others. (Parents are responsible for the growth and nurture of their children. It is thus particularly appropriate that they sponsor their children whom they will nurture in the Christian life. In some cultures this role is undertaken by others in the extended family.)

(iii) The whole Christian community, which on one view is symbolized by the other sponsors and is exemplified by the congregation actually present at the baptism, has a continuing responsibility for nurturing the baptized by prayer, by example, and by support at worship and in their discipleship. This is well expressed in the question addressed to the congregation in several Anglican baptismal rites, "Will you who witness these vows do all in your power to support these persons in their life in Christ?"[6]

(iv) In the baptismal eucharist the infant receives communion along with his or her family.[7]

Administering baptism and communion to very young children properly has consequences for their own Christian growth as well as for the style and conduct of worship. What is needed is an apprehension of the rightful place of baptized children in Christian worship.[8]

The participation of children in the eucharist brings benefits both to the child's immediate family and to the wider family of the church. Children have their own gifts to give. Parental faith is strengthened by the fuller participation of their own children in

God's love. Sharing in the eucharist communicates God's acceptance and love in a powerful way.

In the above pattern we have deliberately not included a formal rite of admission to communion and are concerned that no later rite of admission to communion (nor for that matter confirmation) should take away from the dignity and promise of baptism nor from the commitment of faith implicit in baptism. A child will grow in and express the faith of baptism in a variety of ways through his or her participation in the life and worship of the church.

At some stage it is necessary for the person as an adult to make a responsible faith affirmation in the face of the congregation.[9] How this finds expression varies in different parts of the Anglican Communion. It is normally associated with the laying on of hands by the bishop which may be understood as an acceptance and celebration of all that baptism involved. Within the Anglican Communion other meanings are also associated with laying on of hands and prayer in this context.

Children of nonparticipating parents who regularly come to worship might be dealt with in the following manner. If they are baptized, such children may be admitted to communion after discussion with their parents and with the appointment of sponsors from the congregation. If such children are not baptized it may be helpful to appoint sponsors from the congregation and to enroll the child as a catechumen. After consultation with the parents and preparation this may lead to baptism.

In many parts of the Anglican Communion parochial patterns do not allow a presbyter to be present at every congregation's weekly worship. This may pose additional problems in implementing the communion of all the baptized.

## IV. Recommendations

This Consultation recommends:

   i) that since baptism is the sacramental sign of full incorporation into the church, all baptized persons be admitted to communion.

ii) that provincial baptismal rites be reviewed to the end that such texts explicitly affirm the communion of the newly baptized and that only one rite be authorized for the baptism whether of adults or infants so that no essential distinction be made between persons on basis of age.

iii) that in the celebration of baptism the vivid use of liturgical signs, e.g., the practice of immersion and the copious use of water, be encouraged.

iv) that the celebration of baptism constitute a normal part of an episcopal visit.

v) that anyone admitted to communion in any part of the Anglican Communion be acknowledged as a communicant in every part of the Anglican Communion and not be denied communion on the basis of age or lack of confirmation.[10]

vi) that the Constitution and Canons of each Province be revised in accordance with the above recommendations; and that the Constitution and Canons be amended wherever they imply the necessity of confirmation for full church membership.

vii) that each Province clearly affirm that confirmation is not a rite of admission to communion, a principle affirmed by the bishops at Lambeth in 1968.[11]

viii) that the general communion of all the baptized assume a significant place in all ecumenical dialogues in which Anglicans are engaged.

# Notes

1. In this document "Province" is used to denote a national, regional or autonomous church.

2. *Holy Baptism with Laying-on-of-Hands*, Prayer Book Studies 18 (New York, 1970); *Christian Initiation: The Meaning of Membership*, Canadian Anglican Liturgical Series No. 2 (Toronto, 1970); "The Report of a Provincial Consultation on Confirmation Practice and Experiment to the [New Zealand] General Synod, 1972" (mimeographed); *A Report on Christian Initiation* (1972) and *Report of the Archbishop of Capetown's 1976 Commission on Christian Initiation* (Johannesburg, 1976); *Christian Initiation* (Wales, 1971); and "Liturgical Advisory Committee Report 1976; Confirmation Today" in *Journal of the* [Church of Ireland] *General Synod, 1976*. For an overview of these reports see D. Holeton, "Christian Initiation in Some Anglican Provinces," *Studia Liturgica* 12 (1977): 129-150.

3. The Australian Report of the Commission on Doctrine, "Baptism and Confirmation," in *Proceedings of the Fourth General Synod, 1973*, was an exception to this consensus.

4. *Bonds of Affection: Proceedings of ACC-6* (London, 1984), pp. 53, 70. Our Consultation was held, in part, as a response to the request for continuing study made at ACC-6.

5. This lifelong process of discerning and articulating the rich and diverse meaning of what has been given to the faithful in the sacrament of baptism is referred to as mystagogy.

6. E.g., Book of Common Prayer (United States 1979), p. 303; *Book of Alternative Services* (Canada 1985), p. 155.

7. Experience shows that practical problems are soon solved. A tested practice has been for the minister to dip his or her finger in the chalice and then to allow the infant to suck the wine from the finger. Alternatively, a very small fragment of bread may be moistened with wine and put in the infant's

mouth. Very young children are often best communicated in this way by their parents. Experience has shown that within their first year children learn to extend their hands to receive the bread for themselves.

8. In some places it has been found helpful to have a separate ministry of the word for children from three years to their early teens. At the same time there is considerable room for children to contribute their ministry within the eucharistic liturgy. From an early age children may be involved as readers, intercessors, greeters, servers, acolytes, etc. In formal and informal ways children have an important ministry to exercise within the church.

9. *Baptism, Eucharist and Ministry,* World Council of Churches, Faith and Order Paper No. 111 (Geneva, 1982), Baptism III.8.

10. We note that one Province (Southern Africa) allows for the withdrawal of a child's communicant status in case of permanent removal to a parish other than where the child was admitted to communion. We also note that the Houses of Bishops in the United States and Canada have passed resolutions to ensure that a communicant anywhere in the Anglican Communion is a communicant everywhere within their respective churches.

11. Lambeth Conference 1968, *Resolutions and Reports* (London, 1968), p. 37.

# Participants in the Boston Consultation*

| | | |
|---|---|---|
| The Right Revd. F. A. Amoore | Southern Africa | Provincial Executive Officer, Church of the Province of Southern Africa |
| The Hon. the Revd. Canon Robert Brooks | U.S.A. | Assistant Priest, St. Thomas' Church, Washington, D.C. |
| The Right Revd. Colin Buchanan | England | Bishop of Aston |
| The Right Revd. Brian Davis | New Zealand | Bishop of Waikato |
| The Revd. Ronald Dowling | Australia | Vicar, St. Margaret's Parish, Eltham, Victoria |
| The Revd. Canon Prof. Eugene Fairweather | Canada | Keble Professor of Divinity, Trinity College, Toronto |
| The Revd. Canon Dr. Donald Gray | England | Rector of Liverpool |
| The Revd. Canon Prof. David Holeton | Canada | Assistant Professor of Liturgics and Early Church History, Vancouver School of Theology |
| The Revd. Canon Prof. Leonel Mitchell | U.S.A. | Professor of Liturgics, Seabury-Western Theological Seminary, Evanston, Illinois |
| The Revd. Dr. Kenneth Stevenson | England | Anglican Chaplain and Lecturer in Liturgy, University of Manchester |

*Editor's Note: Participants are listed here with the positions they held at the time of the Consultation in 1985.

| The Revd. Michael Vasey | England | Lecturer in Liturgy, St. John's College, Durham |
| The Revd. Prof. Louis Weil | U.S.A. | Professor of Liturgics and Church Music, Nashotah House, Nashotah, Wisconsin |
| The Revd. Dr. Eugene Brand | Observer | Associate Director, Dept. of Studies, Lutheran World Federation |

# Infant Communion in the
# Episcopal Church

# 13

# Infant Communion: Reflections on the Case from Tradition

*Ruth A. Meyers*

In his article, "Anglican Initiatory Rites: A Contribution to the Current Debate," C. FitzSimons Allison argues against the practice of infant communion on the grounds that it is "anti-biblical, anti-traditional, unpastoral, and counter-productive to mission." In his discussion of tradition, he expresses concern that the "primitive unity" of the rites of initiation in the third century is being imposed upon the contemporary church, and argues that infant communion is not a traditional Anglican practice.[1] Allison's concern about the use of third-century rites as a norm for the contemporary church raises important questions about the role of tradition in shaping current liturgical practice. To address these questions, this article begins with a review of the historical evidence in order to develop an understanding of the evolution of the practice of infant communion throughout the history of the church.

## Historical Background

The first direct evidence of infant communion is found in third-century documents. Prior to this time, the question of whether infants received communion can be answered only indirectly by examining evidence for infant baptism and evidence which indicates that baptism and eucharist formed a single integral rite. The "household baptisms" in Acts (16.14-15, 16.29-34, and 18.8), in which an individual is baptized with his or her family, suggest that children were baptized along with their parents, but the passages do not give any indication as to whether there were infants in those households. In his study of infant baptism,[2] Joachim Jeremias finds that the first definite reference to infant baptism is in Irenaeus, who in about 180 C.E. speaks of "all who through Christ are born again to God, infants and children and boys and young men and old men."[3] The first evidence that baptism and eucharist formed a single integral rite is in Justin Martyr, who in about 150 C.E. describes a rite of baptism which concludes with eucharist.[4] This understanding of baptism and eucharist as a single integral rite suggests that all who were baptized received communion, and that this applied to infants as well as adults.

The description of baptism in *Apostolic Tradition* (dated in the early part of the third century) states, "Baptize the little ones first. All those who can speak for themselves shall do so. As for those who cannot speak for themselves, their parents or someone from their family shall speak for them." Following the baptism, the document describes a eucharist and states that the newly baptized "shall pray together with all the people: they do not pray with the faithful until they have carried out all these things [i.e., baptism]."[5] Here reference to infant baptism and to the baptismal eucharist occurs in the same description of baptism, and presumably all who were baptized received communion.

The earliest direct reference to infant communion is found in Cyprian in about 251. In *De Lapsis,* he speaks of parents who "carried their babies and led their youngsters to be robbed of what they had received in earliest infancy,"[6] and later in the document he tells of an infant who is brought by her parents for communion.[7] The context of these passages is a discussion of the dangers of pagan rites, and it is only incidentally that Cyprian acknowledges a practice of infant communion. Nonetheless it is apparent that, at least in North Africa in the mid-third century, it was customary for infants to receive communion.

In his study of infant communion, the English Evangelical Roger Beckwith cites two third-century texts which he claims indicate that infants and children did not receive communion. The first is from Origen and is dated to about 235:

> Before we arrive at the provision of the heavenly bread, and are filled with the flesh of the spotless Lamb, before we are inebriated with the blood of the true Vine which sprang from the root of David, while we are children, and are fed with milk, and retain the discourse about the first principles of Christ, as children we act under the oversight of stewards, namely the guardian angels.[8]

Beckwith admits that, "Origen's language is highly metaphorical," but he also argues that the passage must refer to "literal children and the literal sacrament."[9] The overall context of this chapter from Origen is not the place of children in the church, but rather the process of maturing in faith. As another example, Origen cites the Israelite crossing of the Red Sea, which was done not under their own power, but through the work of angels. Origen's point is that one begins as a spiritual child, needing the assistance of angels, but must eventually go forth armed to meet the challenges of the world without this same assistance. If this passage is about Christian initiation at all, it most likely refers to an adult catechumenate during which communion was not received rather than a practice of baptized children not receiving communion.

The second passage which Beckwith cites is from the *Didascalia Apostolorum,* an early third-century Syrian document:

> Honor the bishops, who have loosed you from your sins, who by the water regenerated you, who filled you with the Holy Spirit, who reared you with the word as with milk, who bred you up with teaching, who established you with admonition, and made you to partake of the holy eucharist of God, and made you partakers and joint-heirs of the promise of God.[10]

Beckwith argues that the order of this passage indicates that a long course of teaching followed baptism, and only after this instruction were the baptized admitted to communion. However, Beckwith is imposing his model of Christian initiation upon this text, whose context is not a description of the rites of initiation in the Syrian church, but rather a discussion of the role of the bishop.

When these passages are viewed in light of other patristic evidence, it appears that infant communion was not a major theological question during the first three centuries of the church. Believing adults were baptized, and apparently infants and children were included when their families were baptized. Since the pattern of Christian initiation which developed during the first three centuries included a water bath (preceded or followed by an anointing) concluded by eucharist, it follows that all who were baptized, including infants, received communion. As Robert Taft notes in his article on infant communion,

> modern historical research and theological reflection have shown that the universal primitive tradition of both East and West viewed the liturgical completion of Christian Initiation as one integral rite comprising three moments of baptism, chrismation, and eucharist, and without all three the process is incomplete.[11]

Because baptism was considered to be complete only when it was concluded by a eucharist, it is probable that infants who were baptized also received communion. The lack of any discussion of infant communion in patristic literature further suggests that this practice developed without conscious theological reflection.

A single unified rite of Christian initiation was the norm throughout the church in the fourth century and continued to be the sacramental practice and doctrinal teaching of the Western church until the twelfth century. For example, John Chrysostom, in his baptismal catecheses which were preached at Antioch in the late fourth century, describes a baptismal rite which includes anointing, a water bath, and a eucharist,[12] and states that infants are baptized so that they might receive the gifts of "sanctification, justice, filial adoption, and inheritance."[13] Pope Innocent I, in a doctrinal letter in 417, taught that infant initiation necessarily included communion:

> to preach that infants can be given the rewards of eternal life without the grace of baptism is completely idiotic. For unless they eat the flesh of the Son of Man and drink His blood, they will not have life in them.[14]

The actual practice of infant communion is described in early medieval liturgical documents, including the seventh-century *Ordo Romanus XI* and the twelfth-century Roman pontifical:

> Concerning infants, care should be taken lest they receive food or be nursed (except in case of urgent need) before receiving the sacrament of Christ's Body. And afterwards, during the whole of Easter week, let them come to mass, offer, and receive communion every day.[15]

These and other texts make it clear that normative practice throughout the Roman church during the early Middle Ages was for infants to receive communion, and that reception of communion was considered necessary for their salvation.

In his study of Christian initiation in the medieval church, J. D. C. Fisher traces the decline of the practice of infant communion.[16] With the development of a doctrine of sacramental realism, which focused attention upon the eucharistic elements as truly the body and blood of Jesus Christ, concern arose about persons who might not be able to swallow the host. While some began to doubt whether children were proper subjects to receive communion at all, Lanfranc, archbishop of Canterbury during the eleventh century, argued that all persons of all ages needed to receive the Lord's body and blood.[17] Nonetheless, by the twelfth century infants were communicated with wine only, since communion was necessary for their salvation, but they were not able to swallow bread. For example, William of Champeaux wrote in 1121:

> to little children just baptized only the chalice is

given, because they cannot assimilate bread, and in the chalice they receive Christ entire. But the chalice must be given to them, because, as it is impossible for anybody to enter into life without baptism, so is it impossible without this life-giving *viaticum*.[18]

During the eleventh and twelfth centuries, it became increasingly common for the laity to receive only the host. Infants, who were no longer receiving the host, ceased to be communicated with either bread or wine.

While the practice of infant communion declined during the eleventh and twelfth centuries, the age at which children should begin to communicate was not immediately determined. The Fourth Lateran Council, in 1215, ordered yearly confession and communion for all those who had reached the "age of reason," without giving a precise definition of this phrase. Later councils and synods forbade children to communicate until they reached this age of reason, which was defined variously as seven years, ten years, and fourteen years. The effect of these decrees was to associate a person's first reception of communion with the attainment of an indeterminate age of reason, in place of the traditional understanding of communion as the completion of baptism.

This separation of eucharist from baptism was retained by the Anglican reformers of the sixteenth century. Beginning with the 1549 Book of Common Prayer, the "confirmation rubric" ("and there shall none be admitted to the Holy Communion, until such time as he be confirmed") was included in Anglican prayer books. As Allison points out, this rubric originated from Archbishop Peckham in the thirteenth century and was designed not to limit access to communion, but rather to encourage confirmation.[19] Its inclusion in the prayer book meant the continuation of what had become the normative practice of the church. However, a fundamental change occurred in the association of confirmation with education. Prior to the 1549 prayer book, though rare in practice, it was still possible for confirmation to be administered immediately after baptism, of which the best known examples are Prince

Arthur and Princess Elizabeth.[20] The 1549 prayer book changed confirmation to a rite of adolescence by making it conditional upon a certain amount of religious instruction.

The reformers considered it necessary that children learn the essentials of faith, which included the Creed, the Lord's Prayer, and the Ten Commandments. The concluding exhortation in the service of baptism in both the 1549 and 1552 prayer books gives responsibility for this education to the godparents:

> And that they may know these things the better: ye shall call upon them to hear sermons, and chiefly you shall provide that they may learn the Creed, the Lord's Prayer, and the Ten Commandments, in the English tongue: and all other things which a Christian man ought to know and believe to his soul's health.[21]

This education was a prerequisite for confirmation, as the rubrics indicate. Children were required to be able to recite not only the Creed, Lord's Prayer, and Ten Commandments, but also the answers to the questions in the short catechism, which was placed at the beginning of the confirmation service.[22] The requirement that a person be confirmed before receiving communion meant that education also became a prerequisite for receiving communion. This was made explicit in the 1552 prayer book, in which the confirmation rubric was modified to read: "And there shall none be admitted to the Holy Communion, until such time as he can say the Catechism, and be confirmed."[23] Confirmation and first communion were thus associated with education and an individual profession of faith and so became rites of adolescence, while baptism remained a rite of infancy.

This sequence of baptism, confirmation, and first communion did not go unchallenged. David Holeton has shown that the question of infant communion was a central part of the sixteenth- and seventeenth-century debate over infant baptism.[24] The antipedobaptists pointed to the theological inconsistency of admitting infants to baptism but not to eucharist, while the pedobaptists turned to the categories of capacity and faith. Holeton discusses the writings of Jeremy Taylor, who, although a pedobaptist, conceded that infants ought to receive both baptism and eucharist, or neither. Taylor concluded that infant communion was not absolutely necessary, and so the question could be set aside for the sake of unity and peace in the church. The question surfaced again amongst the Nonjurors during the eighteenth century, and Holeton argues that infant communion was normative in their practice until they rejoined the established church at the end of the eighteenth century.[25]

The question of infant communion was not raised again in the Anglican Communion until this century. Resolution 25 of the 1968 Lambeth Conference called upon Anglicans to "explore the theology of baptism and confirmation in relation to the need to commission the laity for their task in the world."[26] The report of the conference suggests that confirmation and admission to communion be separated, and acknowledges the importance of "the intimate relationship of baptism and confirmation with admission to Holy Communion."[27] In their study of the question, the House of Bishops of the Episcopal Church concluded that, "Confirmation should not be regarded as a procedure of admission to the Holy Communion,"[28] while retaining the requirement of education prior to admission to communion.[29] Preliminary versions of the revised rite of baptism included the rubric, "Those who have now been baptized may receive Holy Communion,"[30] which left open the possibility that even newly baptized infants could receive communion.

While this rubric was later eliminated, other rubrics established the principal Sunday eucharist as the normative context for the celebration of baptism, thus linking baptism and eucharist and implying that baptism should conclude with reception of communion. The result has been a variety of practice in the American church, with some parishes communicating newly baptized infants, others giving first communion at a later time (e.g., when the child is old enough to walk to the altar rail; when the child asks to receive communion; after a period of instruction for the child), and some waiting until children are confirmed.

## Infant Communion in the Christian Tradition

The history supports Allison's statement that infant communion is not a traditional Anglican practice. Nevertheless, it was an integral part of the Christian tradition, beginning at least in the fourth, and probably as early as the second, century and continuing until the twelfth century. It was discussed by Anglican theologians during the sixteenth and seventeenth centuries and supported in theory by the well-respected Anglican divine, Jeremy Taylor. It was also practiced by the Nonjurors during the eighteenth century.

In surveying the tradition, it is apparent that the tendency has been for practice to evolve and theological reflection to follow. Thus, infants began to be baptized and receive communion, probably as early as the second century, but substantive theological discussion of the practice first occurs only in the fifth century. By then, the practice was defended as essential for the salvation of infants, and this continued to be true for several centuries. During the eleventh and twelfth centuries, the practice of infant communion died out as a result of sacramental realism and the consequent scrupulosity regarding consecrated bread and wine, yet the theological rationale of an "age of reason" was first discussed in the thirteenth century. During the twentieth century, David Holeton states, "By at least the late 1950s there is evidence that some parochial clergy were communicating children as young as five years old."[31] Yet it is only in light of Lambeth 1968 that this practice began to be officially recognized in Anglicanism. In this century, as previously, theological discussion followed rather than preceded a change in practice. We are presently faced with the continuing spread of a practice of infant communion[32] and ongoing theological debate about the practice.

Recognizing that infant communion has been a part of the Christian tradition does not answer the question of whether it should be practiced in the church today. In his discussion of our contemporary practice, Allison expresses a well-founded concern that we are imposing a third-century model of Christian initiation upon the contemporary church. The third century (or any century) cannot provide a blueprint for our present or our future. Rather, an understanding of our past should free us to respond to our contemporary theological reflection, cultural situation, and pastoral concerns, while maintaining continuity with our Christian roots. As Josef Jungmann points out, "True knowledge of our present liturgy is knowledge based on the solid rock of historical facts; it is by studying the past that we can best learn how to shape the future."[33]

Our present practice of baptism and eucharist reflects this use of our past to help shape our future. The 1979 Book of Common Prayer indicates that "the Holy Eucharist [is] the principal act of Christian worship on the Lord's Day and other major Feasts."[34] This understanding of the centrality of the eucharist is a recovery of practice from the first three centuries of the church, when the Christian community gathered weekly for eucharist. Yet we have not returned to what is understood to be the most primitive form of eucharist, that is, a gathering of the Christian community for a common meal, nor have we copied in minute detail the form of celebrating eucharist during the second and third centuries. Rather, our eucharistic practice reflects centuries of Anglican tradition as well as the practice of the early church.

The restoration of weekly communion in Anglican churches began with the Oxford Movement in the nineteenth century. Massey Shepherd comments,

> By the end of the [nineteenth] century most parishes had a celebration of the Holy Communion every Sunday and holy day, as provided in the Prayer Book, and many of them had one or more celebrations during the week. But the Sunday celebration did not, in many places, become the "principal" parish service more than once a month.[35]

The liturgical revival begun in the nineteenth century has gradually led in this century to the establishment of the weekly parish communion service in many congregations. The Parish Communion movement in England prior to World War II resulted in a shift from Matins to eucharist as the principal Sunday service attended by families.[36] A similar shift has taken place in many places throughout the Anglican Communion, including many parts of the United States.

The development of the weekly parish eucharist is not simply a return to a primitive pattern of Christian celebration, but further reflects a renewed understanding of the centrality of the eucharist in the life of the Christian community. In the introduction to his classic study, *The Shape of the Liturgy,* Gregory Dix states, "Of all Christian 'ritual patterns' that of the eucharist is by common consent central and the most important."[37] In his concluding remarks, he comments on the centrality of the eucharist throughout the history of Christendom:

> best of all, week by week and month by month, on a hundred thousand successive Sundays, faithfully, unfailingly, across all the parishes of Christendom, the pastors have done this [celebrate eucharist] just to *make* the *plebs sancta Dei*—the holy common people of God.[38]

Dix's hyperbole notwithstanding, his comments capture the essence of our renewed understanding of eucharist, that is, eucharist as constitutive of the Christian community.

This renewed understanding of eucharist appears to be directly related to the growing practice of infant communion. David Holeton has noted a similar pattern in the worship of the Nonjurors and of the Catholic Apostolic Church, both of whom understood themselves as communities sustained and nurtured by regular reception of the eucharist, and both of whom had a normative practice of infant communion. He points out, "Whenever the church has come to see itself as a small, gathered, eucharistic community, the communion of all the baptized quickly becomes a real question."[39]

The question of infant communion relates not only to the renewal of eucharistic practice but also to our contemporary theology and practice of baptism. The 1979 prayer book makes it clear that baptism is the only sacrament necessary for full initiation into the church: "Holy Baptism is full initiation by water and the Holy Spirit into Christ's Body the Church."[40] The confirmation rubric has been removed from the prayer book, and the House of Bishops has affirmed that confirmation is not a prerequisite to receiving communion. This has opened the way for all the baptized, including infants, to receive communion.

This renewed understanding of baptism and eucharist has a sound biblical basis. As Acts 2.42 indicates, those who were baptized "devoted themselves to the apostles' teaching and fellowship, to the breaking of the bread and the prayers." Baptism is the sacrament of incorporation into the church, while eucharist, the breaking of the bread, is the central act of the gathered Christian community. Our renewed practice of infant communion arises from the recovery of this biblical understanding of sacraments. Thus infant communion is neither untraditional nor unbiblical, but rather founded upon the New Testament witness to baptism and eucharist, and rooted in Christian tradition.

## The Question of Faith

Allison's objection that infant communion is anti-biblical is based upon his interpretation of 1 Corinthians 11.27-29:

> Whoever eats the bread or drinks the cup of the Lord in an unworthy manner will be guilty of profaning the body and blood of the Lord. Let each person examine oneself, and thus eat of the bread and drink of the cup. For any who eat or drink without discerning the body eat and drink judgment upon themselves.

As Allison acknowledges, the text "does not apply to a child's innocent if ignorant reception, but to a willful and knowledgeable
unworthiness."[41] However, he goes on to raise concern about
modeling reception on ignorance. Allison argues for the primary
importance of responding in faith to the Word of God, which he
calls the cognitive aspect of faith. His argument against infant
communion stems largely from this insistence upon the necessity
of faith which is based upon cognitive understanding.

The association of faith with intellectual understanding is a
legacy from the sixteenth-century Reformation, when education
became a prerequisite for confirmation and the reception of communion. The Reformers were responding to a lack of education on
the part of both laity and clergy and sought to increase the laity's
understanding of the worship of the church. In so doing, faith in
the Anglican tradition became largely dependent upon a cognitive
understanding of Christian doctrine. Other aspects of faith (for
example, faith as trust, faith as an act of the will) were secondary
to the primary importance of cognition. Yet faith involves much
more than intellectual apprehension of Christian teaching.

The experience of faith described throughout the Gospels is a
response to the divine revealed in Jesus. The disciples follow Jesus,
not in response to his teaching, but rather in response to his presence and his command to follow (Mt. 4.18-22; Mk. 1.16-20; Lk.
5.1-11; Jn. 1.35-42; Mt. 9.9). Their act of faith is an act of trust
and obedience, a response of their whole selves to the presence of
the holy revealed in Jesus. Similarly, the woman healed from a flow
of blood by touching the hem of Jesus's garment (Mk. 5.25-34; cf.
Mt. 9.20-22; Lk. 8.43-48) was responding to the divine power she
perceived in Jesus, not to doctrinal formulations. Jesus sends her
on her way, telling her, "Your faith has healed you." Her faith was
belief in Jesus and as such was primarily an act of trust rather than
assent to his teaching.

Faith as an act of personal trust is well-expressed in the resurrection story of Thomas. Thomas refused to believe unless he could

actually touch Jesus's wounds, yet when he was given the opportunity to do so, he responded not by touching but with the words, "My Lord and my God!" Archbishop William Temple comments that Thomas's faith is not based upon his experience in that moment, but

> is grounded in that loyalty which made [him] ready
> to share [his] Master's journey to death. This moment
> has done no more than release a faith which was
> ready, if it could find an occasion, to burst its inhibitions.[42]

Temple describes faith as personal trust. Commenting on John 2.11 ("This, the first of his signs, Jesus did at Cana in Galilee, and manifested his glory; and his disciples believed in him"), Temple says,

> [The disciples] are not here said to believe Him, in
> the sense of believing that what He said was true, but
> to commit themselves to Him in personal trust. This
> is the faith which justifies. To believe true doctrine
> concerning Christ may help us to believe *in* Him; but
> for our spiritual welfare this latter is alone vital.[43]

Paul Tillich, in *Dynamics of Faith*, grapples with the question of what faith is and is not. He begins by saying, "Faith is the state of being ultimately concerned."[44] Ultimate concern is both the basis for every act of faith and the object of each act of faith. It is much more than a matter of belief in a creed or doctrinal principles, but is an act of the whole self, including cognition, will, and emotion. Tillich writes:

> in every act of faith there is cognitive affirmation, not
> as the result of an independent process of inquiry but
> as an inseparable element in a total act of acceptance
> and surrender....There is certainly affirmation by the
> will of what concerns one ultimately, but faith is not a
> creation of the will....Faith is not an emotional out-
> burst: this is not the meaning of ecstasy...emotion
> does not produce faith.[45]

In his study of faith development, James Fowler draws upon Tillich and other theologians, as well as developmental psychologists such as Piaget, Erikson, and Kohlberg. Fowler identifies stages of faith development through which individuals progress throughout their lifetime. The stages relate to each person's age and life experiences. Fowler finds that faith is present in individuals in different ways, depending upon their developmental stage. Underlying all stages of faith is the basic experience of faith as trust, a capacity which is present at birth and which begins to develop as soon as a child begins interacting with those around her, that is, also at birth. In his introduction, Fowler writes:

> We are endowed at birth with nascent capacities for faith. How these capacities are activated and grow depends to a large extent on how we are welcomed into the world and what kinds of environments we grow in. Faith is interactive and social; it requires community, language, ritual and nurture. Faith is also shaped by initiatives from beyond us and other people, initiatives of spirit or grace. How these latter initiatives are recognized and imaged, or unperceived and ignored, powerfully affects the shape of faith in our lives.[46]

All people spend their entire lifetime maturing in their faith. The capacity for faith, present at birth, develops and is given expression as the person interacts with her world.

The church in baptizing infants incorporates them into a community in which they can develop further the personal trust which is the basis of faith and in which their faith can be nurtured. In the words of the catechism, "Infants are baptized so that they can share citizenship in the Covenant, membership in Christ, and redemption by God."[47] Parents and sponsors are expected to bring the child up in the church, where the child learns to follow and know Christ. The church also has a responsibility to provide an environment which permits each person's faith to develop as the person grows and matures. To encourage Christian faith to develop requires a community in which each person can come to commit herself to Christ in personal trust. As William Temple has written, this is the development of a belief in Christ rather than assent to teaching about Christ.

## Conclusion

The reception of communion is dependent upon faith, as the catechism states: "The inward and spiritual grace in the Holy Communion is the Body and Blood of Christ given to his people, and *received by faith*."[48] Fowler's work has shown that faith is a capacity present in all people from birth. The church recognizes this capacity in baptizing infants, thus incorporating them into the faith community. To admit them to the sacrament which is the central act in the ongoing life of that community, that is, the eucharist, is to offer the means by which infants, and all people, can be nurtured in their faith.

While education is an important aspect of growth in faith, it is only one part of faith development. The Christian community must be a community in which all people are continually being formed in the Christian faith and life and encouraged to develop the faith which is appropriate to their age and life experience. As the constitutive act of the Christian community, communion of all the baptized is a primary means by which all Christians are nurtured in this faith, faith which is an ever deepening personal trust in Jesus, a faith which proclaims, "My Lord and my God!" in response.

## Notes
1. *Anglican and Episcopal History* 56 (1987): 27-43.
2. Joachim Jeremias, *Infant Baptism in the First Four Centuries* (E.T., London: S.C.M., 1960), and *The Origins of Infant Baptism* (E.T., London: S.C.M., 1963).
3. *Against Heresies* 2:22:4, or 2:33:2.

4. Justin Martyr, *First Apology* 65.1-3.

5. Geoffrey Cuming, *Hippolytus: A Text for Students* (Bramcote, Nott.: Grove Books, 1976), pp. 18-21.

6. Cyprian, *De Lapsis,* 9.

7. Ibid., 25.

8. Origen, *Homilies on the Book of Judges* 6:2.

9. "The Age of Admission to the Lord's Supper," *Westminster Theological Journal* 38 (1976): 126.

10. *Didascalia Apostolorum,* ch. 9.

11. Robert Taft, "On the Question of Infant Communion in the Byzantine Catholic Churches of the U.S.A.," *Diakonia* 17 (1982): 201-214. Taft cites as representative studies Aidan Kavanagh, *The Shape of Baptism: The Rite of Christian Initiation,* (New York: Pueblo, 1978), and Mark Searle, *Christening: The Making of Christians* (Collegeville, Minn.: Liturgical Press, 1980).

12. Baptismal Catecheses, Stavronikita Series, 2.27.

13. Ibid., 3.6.

14. *Ep.* 30, 5. *PL* 20, 592, cited by Taft, p. 208.

15. M. Andrieu, ed., *Le pontifical romain au moyen age,* vol. 1 (*Studi e testi* 86, Vatican 1938) p. 248:37, cited by Taft, p. 208.

16. J. D. C. Fisher, *Christian Initiation: Baptism in the Medieval West,* Alcuin Club Collections 47 (London: SPCK, 1965), pp. 101-108. Fisher's discussion is summarized in this article.

17. Ibid., p. 102.

18. *Frag.*; *PL* 163, 1039, cited by Fisher, pp. 102-103.

19. Allison, p. 27.

20. Henry Holloway, *The Confirmation and Communion of Infants and Young Children* (London, 1901), p. 44, cited by Richard L. DeMolen, "Childhood and the Sacraments in the Sixteenth Century," *Archiv für Reformationsgeschichte* 66 (1975):54.

21. "Of the Administracion of Publyke Baptisme to be used in the Church," *First and Second Prayer Books of Edward VI,* Everyman's Library (London, J. M. Dent and Sons, 1960), pp. 241, 402.

22. *First and Second Prayer Books,* pp. 247-250, 404-408.

23. "Confirmacion," *First and Second Prayer Books,* p. 409.

24. David R. Holeton, "Communion of All the Baptized and Anglican Tradition," *Anglican Theological Review* 69 (1987):13-22. Reprinted above, pp. 19-41; references below are to the original article.

25. Ibid., pp. 23-24.

26. Lambeth Conference 1968, *Resolutions and Reports* (London: SPCK, 1968), p. 37.

27. Ibid., p. 99.

28. Report of the Special Meeting of the House of Bishops, 1971, in *Journal of the General Convention of...the Episcopal Church,* 1973, p. 1073.

29. "We further recommend that no child be admitted to Holy Communion unless instructed in the meaning of this sacrament" (ibid., p. 1063).

30. Prayer Book Studies 26 (New York: Church Hymnal Corp., 1973), p. 16. See also Prayer Book Studies 18 (New York: Church Pension Fund, 1970), p. 40.

31. Holeton, "Communion of All the Baptized," p. 25.

32. David Holeton, *Infant Communion—Then and Now,* Grove Liturgical Studies 27 (Bramcote, Nott.: Grove Books, 1981), pp. 22-26.

33. J. A. Jungmann, *The Early Liturgy to the Time of Gregory the Great,* trans. Francis A. Brunner (London: Darton, Longman & Todd, 1960), p. 8. For further discussion of the use of tradition, see Paul Bradshaw, "The Liturgical Use and Abuse of Patristics," in Kenneth Stevenson, ed., *Liturgy Reshaped*

(London: SPCK, 1982), pp. 134-145; and Robert Taft, "On the Question of Infant Communion."

34. Book of Common Prayer 1979, p. 13.

35. Massey H. Shepherd, *The Worship of the Church,* The Church's Teaching Series, Vol. 4 (Greenwich, Conn.: Seabury, 1952), p. 149.

36. For a detailed history of the Parish Communion movement, see Donald Gray, *Earth and Altar: The Evolution of the Parish Communion in the Church of England to 1945,* Alcuin Club Collections 68 (Norwich: Canterbury Press, 1986).

37. Gregory Dix, *The Shape of the Liturgy* (London: A & C Black, 1945; Seabury Edition, New York: Seabury, 1982), p. xi.

38. Ibid., p. 744.

39. Holeton, "Communion of All the Baptized," p. 27.

40. Book of Common Prayer 1979, p. 298.

41. Allison, p. 37.

42. William Temple, *Readings in St. John's Gospel* (London: Macmillan and Co., 1940), p. 391.

43. Ibid., p. 37.

44. Paul Tillich, *Dynamics of Faith* (New York: Harper & Row, 1957), p. 1.

45. Ibid., p. 7.

46. James W. Fowler, *Stages of Faith: The Psychology of Human Development and the Quest for Meaning* (San Francisco: Harper & Row, 1981), p. xiii.

47. Book of Common Prayer 1979, p. 858.

48. Ibid., p. 859. Emphasis added.

# 14

# The Communion of Infants and Little Children

*Leonel L. Mitchell*

In nothing has the Liturgical Movement of the twentieth century made so visible an impact on the life of the Episcopal Church as in the place of the Holy Eucharist in the Sunday schedules of our parishes and in the worship habits of our members. While it is true that the Catholic revival associated with the Oxford Movement in the nineteenth century made the weekly celebration of the eucharist normative in Anglicanism, this frequently took the form of an "early Communion service" without music or preaching attended by "the devout," early risers, and those determined to avoid music, preaching or both. The usual worship experience of Episcopalians was either choral Morning Prayer or, in Anglo-Catholic parishes, high mass, at which the majority of the congregation did not communicate. It remained for the twentieth-century Liturgical Movement to make what Gabriel Hebert called "the Parish Communion"[1] a fixture in the majority of Episcopal congregations.

### The Family Eucharist

Increasingly today Episcopalians attend a Sunday celebration of the eucharist with both music and preaching, with the general communion of the entire congregation. This service is usually known as "the Parish Eucharist" or "the Family Eucharist." It is held weekly as "the principal act of Christian worship on the

Lord's Day."[2] Families are urged to attend together, and participation in the service is frequently an integral part of the parish Christian education program for both children and adults.

The unaccustomed phenomenon of the general weekly reception of communion by the vast majority of churchgoers has raised the question of who is eligible to receive communion in a new way. It is no longer simply an interesting theological discussion. It is a hotly controversial pastoral question. As long as most worshipers did not, in fact, receive communion very often the question of the communion of infants and children could easily be avoided. Often the children did not attend church, but participated in a separate children's service, at which there was no expectation that anyone would communicate, nor indeed any opportunity to do so. Even if children did attend an occasional eucharistic celebration, the fact that many, often most, members of the congregation did not communicate would take the "sting" out of their exclusion from communion. Usually, children did not expect to receive communion. They had been taught that this was a privilege reserved for the confirmed.

## Non-Communicating Attendance

The voluntary non-reception of communion by lay people has been commented upon and condemned by church leaders from the time of John Chrysostom.[3] Calvin, for example, taught that all church members should communicate every Sunday.[4] His inability to convince lay people, including members of the Geneva town council, of this is one of the principal causes of the loss of regular Sunday eucharistic worship among the Reformed. Cranmer, like Calvin, saw general communion at a weekly celebration of the eucharist as the ideal,[5] but did not succeed in making the practice normative for Anglicanism in the centuries following. It has only been in the second half of the twentieth century that the ideal of weekly communion has begun to be realized even among the minority of Christians who actually attend weekly worship. This restoration is soundly based in the praxis and teaching of the ancient church,[6] and, for Anglicans, represents putting into practice not only the provisions of the 1979 prayer book but also the implied teaching of every prayer book since 1549. A beginning has thus been made in closing the gap between the teaching and the practice of the Episcopal Church, at least in this area.

Even more than the restoration of weekly eucharistic worship, the restoration of general weekly communion has run up against entrenched and long-standing contrary custom, some of it established for a millennium. This results not only in the gap between the liturgy's assumption that Christians will desire to communicate weekly and the rubrical or canonical establishment of a minimum number of times per year one must communicate in order to remain "a communicant in good standing,"[7] but also in the development of a body of custom which simply assumes that communion will be an infrequent, although important, event.

## The Blessing of Non-Communicants

The question of the communion of young children in the Episcopal Church appeared, then, as a pastoral issue. Large numbers of children attending the parish eucharist with their parents were brought forward by them to the communion rail. The custom developed of the priest giving a blessing to the children while communicating the adults. Although well intentioned, intending to avoid the embarrassing appearance of ignoring the very children whom the clergy had urged the parents to bring, it raised serious theological questions.

What is the significance of a priestly blessing of a non-communicant? In the ancient church it was the practice for the bishop to bless those who were being dismissed before the liturgy of the faithful.[8] These included catechumens of various classes, those possessed by demons, and penitents not yet readmitted to communion. All of these groups were prayed for by the congregation and departed with the bishop's blessing immediately before the prayers of the faithful. Some clergy, mistakenly identifying baptized children with the unbaptized adult catechumens of the early church, adopted the custom of dismissing children to go to Sunday School classes after the liturgy of the word. Others, recognizing that children as baptized church members should participate in the eucharistic liturgy itself, had the children remain until the time of the communion of the people and either dismissed them as a group with a blessing or gave individual blessings to children as they came forward to the communion rail with their parents. In the medieval Gallican rite the custom had arisen of having the bishop bless those "communicants" who were departing without receiving communion. This was done after the celebrant's communion. It is the source of our traditional final blessing by the celebrant.[9] This has also been cited as a precedent for blessing non-communicating children.

### Turning Away Those Who Come Forward

Whether it is good theology to adopt another era's pastoral response to the problem of adult communicants being unwilling to communicate and apply it to modern children is at best problematical. Even more problematical is the question of the right by which a celebrant (whether priest or bishop) refuses to communicate a baptized person who desires to receive communion. The prayer book provides a series of "disciplinary rubrics"[10] stating the circumstances under which this may be done. They apply to those who are "living a notoriously evil life," to those who "have done wrong to their neighbors and are a scandal to the other members of the congregation," and to those who hate and refuse to forgive other members of the congregation. In my experience very few of these people are infants or young children. Age is nowhere given as a criterion for refusing to communicate anyone.

### Communion of All the Baptized

The historical process by which the universal tradition of the church for the first thousand years that baptized members of all ages should communicate fell into desuetude has been well set forth by J. D. C. Fisher in *Christian Initiation: Baptism in the Medieval West*,[11] and more recently by Ruth A. Meyers, in the July 1988 issue of *Anglican and Episcopal History*.[12] The significant fact is that there was no theologically based decision to stop the communion of infants. It simply fell as a casualty to the denial of the chalice to lay people. Infants who could not chew the consecrated bread were communicated with the consecrated wine alone, as is still done in the Byzantine rite.[13] If there was a reason for the lapse of communion of infants it was none of those suggested by Bishop Allison,[14] but fear born of an overly realistic late medieval view of Christ's presence in the elements lest children should profane the sacrament by "spitting up," as infants are wont to do.

### Generally Necessary to Salvation

Ever since the introduction of the section on the sacraments in the revision of Cranmer's catechism for the English prayer book of 1604 the Anglican church has in one way or another been making this thoroughly sound theological statement:

> Two [sacraments] only, as generally necessary to salvation, that is to say, Baptism and the Supper of the Lord.[15]

Yet there has been a gap between the clear statement of this principle and our practical insistence that this only applies to "those of riper years." Considering the proclaimed dominical character and general necessity of the two Gospel sacraments,[16] to require anything else as a condition for the reception of one of them seems dangerously close to leaving the commandment of God and holding fast to human traditions.[17]

The question of who may receive communion is not principally canonical and pastoral, but profoundly theological. It has to do with the nature of baptism and eucharist, their relationship to each other and to the paschal mystery of our participation in the death and resurrection of Jesus Christ. It is not ultimately a question of what the congregation likes, or can be coerced into enduring, or even of pastoral concern for families, but of the nature of the church, of the sacraments, and of the salvation won once for all by Jesus Christ.

## The Paschal Unity of Baptism and Eucharist

The sacrament of holy baptism constitutes us as the people of the New Covenant, uniting us to Jesus the high priest and establisher of the Covenant. The eucharist is the Covenant meal in which the people of God eat and drink proleptically at God's table in the eternal Kingdom. The two sacraments are a unity. Historically the eucharist forms the climax and conclusion of the rite of Christian initiation. The Russian Orthodox theologian Alexander Schmemann writes:

> In the real Orthodox tradition...the *metabole* itself—the change of the bread and wine into the Body and Blood of Christ—and the communion of the Holy Gifts are viewed as the fulfillment, the crowning point and the climax, of the whole eucharistic liturgy, whose meaning is precisely that it *actualizes* the Church as new creation, reconciled with God, given access to heaven, filled with divine Glory, sanctified by the Holy Spirit, and *therefore* capable of and called to participation in divine Life, in the communion of the Body and Blood of Christ...
>
> Clearly only such understanding and experience of the Eucharist reveals it as the self-evident and necessary fulfillment of Baptism...If Eucharist is truly *the sacrament of the Church*...then of necessity to enter the Church is to enter into the Eucharist, then Eucharist is indeed the fulfillment of Baptism...
>
> Of all this the newly baptized have been made participants and partakers. They were baptized so that hav-

ing died with Christ they might partake of His Risen Life, and it is this Risen Life that the Eucharist manifests and communicates in the Church, making her members into witnesses of the things to come.[18]

Our earliest account, in Justin Martyr, concludes its description of the baptismal washing by saying:

> We, however, after thus washing the one who has been convinced and signified his assent, lead him to those who are called brethren, where they are assembled. They then earnestly offer common prayers for themselves and the one who has been illuminated, and all others everywhere, that we may be made worthy....On finishing the prayers we greet each other with a kiss. Then bread and a cup of water and mixed wine are brought to the president of the brethren....When the president has given thanks and the whole congregation has assented, those whom we call deacons give *to each of those present* a portion of the consecrated bread and wine and water....[19]

Baptism and eucharist comprised a single whole. The reception of communion by the newly baptized with the rest of the congregation was, in fact, the final repeatable act of the rite, which signified that every time the neophytes received communion for the remainder of their lives it would be the renewal of the baptismal covenant, their participation in the paschal mystery of the dying and rising again of Jesus Christ. There is ample evidence that this union of baptism and eucharist was in no way dependent upon the age of the neophytes. John the Deacon, writing from Rome about the year 500, describes the communion of the newly baptized and comments:

> I must say plainly and at once, in case I seem to have overlooked the point, that all these things are done even to infants, who by reason of their youth understand nothing.[20]

The seventh-century *Ordo Romanus XI* says, following the baptism and chrismation:

> After this they go in to Mass and all the infants receive communion. Care is to be taken lest after they have been baptized they receive any food or sucking before they communicate.[21]

In the Byzantine liturgy, the unity of baptism and eucharist upon which Schmemann so glowingly commented above, which John Chrysostom clearly describes in his baptismal homilies,[22] and which is found in the earliest Byzantine liturgical book, the Barbarini Euchologion,[23] is no longer apparent in the present rite. A vestige of the link is maintained, however, by concluding the baptismal rite with a paschal procession and word liturgy and communicating the neophyte from the reserved sacrament.[24] So the tradition of communicating the newly baptized is maintained, even though the union of baptism and eucharist has been lost.

## Two Levels of Church Membership

To set some sort of sacramental test between baptism and communion, whether it be confirmation or an act of personal adult commitment to Christ, results almost inevitably in producing what, in fact, Anglicans have had for centuries, two levels of membership. The largest group are the baptized members, whereas the smaller circle of communicants appears as an elite core group. There seems no way to avoid either falling into Pelagianism and admitting that receiving communion is a reward for personal achievement, usually intellectual rather than spiritual, not the food of all of the people of God, or, on the other hand, retreating from the clear teaching of The Book of Common Prayer that "Holy Baptism is full initiation by water and the Holy Spirit into Christ's Body the Church,"[25] into a position like that of Gregory Dix, by insisting that something more is required for *real* communicant membership. It is justification, not by faith, but by intellectual accomplishment.

## Children Are a Sign to the Adult Community

Allison comments in his article mentioned above:

> It is not necessarily superstitious to communicate, *for pastoral reasons,* infants, or those whose consciousness is impaired. But it is likely to evoke superstition when the practice of receiving in ignorance becomes the normal policy of the church.[26]

I may do the bishop a disservice, but my interpretation of "for pastoral reasons" is that there is no *proper theological reason* to communicate infants or the mentally handicapped, but that it is all right to do so to keep from hurting people's feelings. It would seem to me, on the contrary, that there is no better sign of the unmerited gracious gift of God to humankind in the holy sacrament of the altar than its gift to those who clearly do not and cannot "merit" it. It reminds us that we are all called to be like children if we would enter the kingdom of heaven.

Ignorance in the sense of unwillingness to learn is not at question here, but rather inexperience, innocence, and the inability to comprehend. Yet compared to the truth of the mystery of redemption, the difference between what I understand and what the infant understands is as the difference in distance between leaving from New York and leaving from Tokyo on a trip to Mars. While from my earthbound perspective it may appear large, it is but a tiny fraction of the total.

I know of no one suggesting that learning to "give a reason for the faith that is in you"[27] is not incumbent upon those who would grow in grace as they grow in knowledge. Indeed, I, like other contemporary liturgists, have always specifically stated that the religious formation and education of children is a principal task and function of the local Christian community. There is always the danger implicit in any church which initiates infants that their membership will remain on an infantile basis and church membership in general will come to be purely nominal, while in churches which restrict membership to "those who believe" there is the danger of Pelagian elitism, the development of an Anabaptist ecclesiology which sees the visible church as a voluntary association of consenting adults, and the abandonment of the form of "the church" for that of "a sect." The suggestion that it is appropriate to baptize infants but not to communicate them is an unscriptural and untraditional attempt to "get the best of both worlds" and, like all such compromises, frequently gets the worst of them instead.

The reason, then, for communicating infants and small children is the same as the reason for communicating anyone else. It is a sign of the kingdom, of their membership in the new people of God, of their participation in the life of the Risen One. It would seem to me to be most important theologically to do this on the occasion of their baptism, to insist, with Schmemann, that the eucharist is *the* sign of the risen life into which the neophytes have been born. It is the sacramental sign that they are indeed "members incorporate in the mystical body" of Jesus Christ. To refuse to communicate them appears to proclaim that there is some significant sense in which they are *not* really members. This is, of course, exactly the two-tiered membership approach which confirmation has fostered in most Western churches, distinguishing "baptized members" from "communicants."

## Children as Church Members

It is certainly true that in any family or community there are activities to which simple membership does not admit you. Children are not normally given decision-making roles, for example, but participation in meals at the family table is not normally denied them. An understanding of nutrition is not a prerequisite for eating. John Frederick has forcefully reminded us that the participation of children in the eucharist is a sign primarily not to the children but to the gathered community:

> Their inclusion in either covenant was never ruled
> out because they could not "understand"—even idiots
> can be Christians. Indifference to infant membership

tells us more about lack of community awareness than it does about God...

The inclusion of those who show the greatest changes in their development is particularly apt when the world is tempted to repudiate change, not knowing what to make of it. In this setting for the Church to harp on "commitment" is futile. It is an unpaschal yearning for arrival characteristics which, if allowed to intrude unduly into covenant principles of membership, threatens to undo the covenant community's signification of its paschal Lord. Fastening upon explicit acts of faith as the sole indication of authentic commitment betrays a failure to appreciate the covenant community's relationships as these witness to Jesus Christ. An adult style of commitment is no more proper to the renewal of membership in eucharist than it is proper to the bestowal of membership in baptism...[28]

While it is hard to see why reception of the sacrament of holy communion should be necessary only for adults, the primary reason for communicating infants is not for the benefit of the infants but for that of the church. The child is a witness to the community. This witness is most eloquently borne when all neophytes, regardless of age, receive communion at their baptism. This, I believe, is the place to start. To administer communion to a baby at his or her baptism is to bear witness before the world to this child's membership in the people of God. The child is washed and fed at the Lord's Table as a child of God. I do not know what the inner significance of those events are to the child. Certainly as children grow in wisdom and stature the meaning will become more evident to them. But from the beginning God is acting in and through them, in the water of baptism and in the bread and wine of the eucharist. They are grafted into the body of Christ, nourished and brought to maturity within it, surrounded by the grace of God.

## The Force of Contrary Custom

I remain uncertain as to the basis upon which a Christian pastor can refuse to communicate such a little one. Our custom, however, is different, and custom is powerful. Until the General Convention of 1970 the Episcopal Church forbade the communicating of the unconfirmed by the "confirmation rubric."[29] Although historically this rubric was not intended to forbid the communicating of infants and young children, but rather to encourage their confirmation, it had the effect of enforcing the excommunication of unconfirmed children.[30]

## A Change in Discipline

It is undeniably true that the admission of baptized infants and young children to communion represents a change in the *discipline* of the Episcopal Church. However many patristic, medieval Eastern and Western, and contemporary Eastern sources are cited, the fact remains that this has not been Anglican custom since 1549, nor has it been the custom of "main line" American churches. It is the present writer's contention that it does not represent a change in the *doctrine* of the Episcopal Church. Even the Council of Trent did not go so far as to claim that there were theological objections to the communion of infants, but only that "little children who do not have the use of reason *are not under any obligation* to receive the Eucharist in sacramental communion."[31]

The resolutions of the General Convention of 1970 and the House of Bishops in 1971 are the first legislative fruit of a change in thinking about the communion of children among Anglicans which had been reflected in Resolution 25 of the Lambeth Conference of 1968.[32] This change was not brought about by the 1979 prayer book but reflected in it, and it is certainly true that the removal of the "confirmation rubric" from that book brought this matter to the attention of many who had never considered it before.

The occasion for the resolutions of General Convention was the submission to them of Prayer Book Studies 18, *Holy Baptism with the Laying-on-of-Hands*.[33] This study contained the unambiguous rubric, "Those who have now been christened may receive Holy Communion,"[34] and its introduction included the straightforward statement, "It is anticipated that Holy Communion will be administered to all who have been baptized at this service: by ancient custom, infants are communicated from a spoon or by intinction."[35]

The authorization of the rite of Prayer Book Studies 18 was severely limited by the enabling resolution cited above, which authorized the use of only the baptismal section of the rite by a priest and forbade children "under the present normal age for confirmation" from receiving the Laying-on-of-Hands, even from the bishop "during the trial use period." It was, nevertheless, this resolution which permitted the communion of unconfirmed children "subject to the direction and guidance of the Ordinary."[36]

The principal concern of the bishops was not the communion of infants, but the "confirmation" of infants and the permission given to priests to "confirm." Pursuant to Canon II.3.6(c) the Presiding Bishop (John E. Hines) and the President of the House of Deputies (John B. Coburn) authorized for trial use adaptations of the rite made by the Standing Liturgical Commission at their meeting of February 19-22, 1971.[37] These adaptations provided a substitute prayer to be used at the chrismation when a priest presided and directions for use of the Laying-on-of-Hands by the bishop as a "confirmation service" without baptisms, and for the bishop to baptize children without the laying on of hands. The administration of communion to children is not mentioned in the document, for this was not the Convention's primary concern. They feared confirmation was being abolished.[38]

As a result of these actions of General Convention and the Standing Liturgical Commission, unconfirmed children began to receive communion in the Episcopal Church. Different Ordinaries, of course, gave different "guidance and direction." In some dioceses infants were regularly communicated at their baptism and whenever they came forward to receive subsequently. In others, the Roman Catholic "first communion class" for seven year olds made its appearance. Still others did nothing.

The Standing Liturgical Commission, for its part, prepared a revision of the rites of Christian initiation, Prayer Book Studies 26.[39] This study also provided for the communion of the newly baptized by a rubric stating, "Those who have now been baptized may receive Holy Communion."[40] Daniel Stevick, a member of the drafting committee, edited a Supplement to Prayer Book Studies 26, which was issued under his name. It contained a discussion of first communion and a defense of its reassociation with baptism.[41]

## Discipline in Transition

Throughout the period of "trial use" from 1970 to 1976, the materials before the Episcopal Church clearly *expected*, but did not *require*, the communion of the newly baptized at the baptismal eucharist. It was this practice which was theologically consistent with the rites proposed, but it was recognized that many people in the Episcopal Church, including bishops and deputies to General Convention, had never considered the question. In any event, the rubric does not appear in The Book of Common Prayer 1979. It was eliminated between the 1975 revision of the proposed rite[42] and its appearance in *The Draft Proposed Book of Common Prayer* of February 2, 1976.[43] At the time, the reason given for its removal was that it was believed by some to be a surreptitious attempt to "open" communion in the Episcopal Church to baptized members of other churches.[44] The result of this is that no statement appears in the prayer book requiring baptism as a prerequisite for receiving communion, although the church clearly does so teach and act.

At the General Convention of 1988 a proposed order for "The Preparation of Parents and Godparents for the Baptism of Infants and Young Children" for inclusion in *The Book of Occasional*

*Services* was presented from the Standing Liturgical Commission. As proposed it contained this section concerning the actual baptism of the children:

> In accordance with the Book of Common Prayer, this will take place on a major baptismal day at the principal service of worship. The infant will be signed (with chrism, if desired) and *will* receive Holy Communion (in the form of a few drops of wine if it is not yet weaned). [emphasis added]

The phrase "*will* receive Holy Communion" was amended by the Convention to "*may* receive."[45] This seems to be a good barometer of where the Episcopal Church is today on the subject of the communion of infants and small children. It is no longer an exotic phenomenon. The argument has moved from, "Is it permissible for young children to receive communion?" to "Is it absolutely necessary for them to do so?" The Convention has said that it is not, but it has equally certainly affirmed that it is a reasonable and authorized practice.

## Conclusion

The Episcopal Church affirms the theological principle that baptism admits to communion. This is not a new principle, but one which we have affirmed but not practiced over the years. The prayer book categorically rejects the suggestion that there are levels of membership in the church. The baptized are church members *tout simple*. True, the catechism speaks of requirements for the reception of communion: "that we should examine our lives, repent of our sins, and be in love and charity with all people,"[46] as it requires of those who come to be baptized "...that we renounce Satan, repent of our sins, and accept Jesus as our Lord and Savior."[47] Clearly infants can no more do the one than the other. There seems to be no basis in scripture or reason and only a limited and late (if recently all prevailing) basis in tradition for assuming that the church as a corporate body can undertake to do these things for infants at the font but not at the table.

The two sacraments of the paschal mystery which incorporate us into Jesus Christ dying and rising again should not be rent asunder. Participation in the eucharist as a communicant is the natural conclusion of the initiatory rite, for it is this that is the sign and seal of our membership in Christ. They are related as birth is related to life.

I believe that it is important to assert this and to encourage the communicating of all the newly baptized at their baptism and to affirm their right as church members to receive the sacraments and other rites and ceremonies of the church. A dying child, for example, should be communicated and receive the rites for the sick.

Whether it is pastorally desirable to bring all baptized children to the altar to receive communion weekly, monthly, or even yearly, as is the custom in many Eastern Orthodox churches, is surely a practical pastoral question, the answer to which may differ from congregation to congregation, as long as it is recognized that the child may not be forbidden to receive.

The dangers in taking any other position are real. Communion comes to be viewed as a "good work," something which we must "merit" in order to receive. Communicants become an elite group within the membership, and, in Calvin's wonderful phrase, "a half of the efficacy of baptism is lopt off,"[48] and the church itself becomes not the family of God, but a club for the pious who choose to join.

There is, of course, the danger inherent in any church that practices infant baptism. Membership may become routine and nominal, lacking the enthusiasm of the committed converts of sects which initiate only adult converts, although the more "churchlike" these sects become the less actual difference in the commitment of members there turns out to be. Our previous practice of delaying first communion until adolescence did not save us from that danger, and communicating infants will certainly not do so either. It will, however, have the advantage of putting our praxis in line with our theology and treating all of the baptized as members of the church, maintaining the unity of the Gospel sacraments, and putting ourselves in the position of being able to see the children in our midst as the signs that Jesus showed them to be of membership in the heavenly kingdom as the unmerited gift of God's grace.

## Notes

1. See Donald Gray, *Earth and Altar*, Alcuin Club Collections 68 (Norwich: Canterbury Press, 1986), pp. 198-200.

2. The Book of Common Prayer, 1979 (hereafter BCP), p. 13.

3. Chrysostom, *Homilies on Ephesians* 3, trans. *The Nicene and Post-Nicene Fathers* (New York: Christian Literature Co., 1896), Vol. 13, p. 64ff:

   In vain is the daily sacrifice, in vain do we stand before the Altar; there is no one to partake...    Look, I entreat: a royal table is set before you. Angels minister at the table, the King himself is there, and dost thou stand gaping?...For everyone that partaketh not of the mysteries, is standing here in shameless effrontery.

4. John Calvin, *Institutes of the Christian Religion*, 4, 17, 43-44, trans. F. L. Battles, ed. John T. McNeill, Library of the Christian Classics 21 (Philadelphia: Westminster Press, 1960), pp. 1421ff:

   The Supper could have been administered more becomingly if it were set before the church very often, and at least once a week...and in becoming order the believers should partake of the most holy banquet, the ministers breaking the bread and giving the cup....And in those old canons which they call "apostolic" we read: "Those who do not stay until the end, and do not receive the sacred communion, should be corrected as disturbers of the church." In the council of Antioch [341 C.E.], also, it was decreed that those who enter the church and hear the Scriptures and abstain from communion should be removed from the church until they correct this fault. Obviously, by these constitutions holy men meant to retain and protect the frequent practice of communion, received, as it was, from the apostles themselves. For they saw that it was most wholesome for believers but that it gradually fell into disuse out of common neglect.

5. This is the obvious meaning of the provisions of both the First and Second Prayer Books of Edward VI. The Communion was to be the normal Sunday service. The first prayer book speaks of "dailie Communion" as normal in cathedrals and "other places." It calls for the other clergy resident in the parish to assist the chief celebrant and to receive communion. It provides an exhortation to be used "if upon the Sunday or holy day the people be negligent to come to the Communion" to encourage them to do so (Brightman, *The English Rite*, [London: Rivingtons, 1921], Vol. II, p. 658).

6. The evidence of the early church is overwhelming and unanimous. As careful and conservative a scholar as C. F. D. Moule could write, "There appears to be sufficient evidence for believing that, from, the earliest days, a sacrament such as came to be called the Holy Communion or Eucharist was celebrated, probably weekly, and usually in the context of a meal" (*Worship in the New Testament,* Ecumenical Studies in Worship 9 [Richmond: John Knox Press, 1961], p. 29). By the beginning of the second century Justin Martyr can assert confidently that there is an assembly of the Christians in each place "on the day called Sunday" which includes the reading and preaching of the Scripture, the celebration of the eucharist, and the reception of the consecrated elements "by each one." Moreover, "they are sent to the absent by the deacons" (*I Apology* 67).

7. The English prayer books of both 1552 and 1662, for example, state, "Every parishioner shall communicate at the least three times in the year, of which Easter to be one" (Brightman, *The English Rite*, p. 719). The Canons of the

Episcopal Church maintain this rule (I.17.2). The Fourth Lateran Council had required communion only at Easter, although other medieval regulations spoke also of Christmas and Pentecost. The 1549 prayer book had similarly required "every man and woman...to communicate once in the year at the least" (Brightman, p. 718). It is at least interesting that the 1552 and 1662 prayer books require "every parishioner" to communicate, not every *confirmed* parishioner, as the "confirmation rubric" might lead one to expect, nor every parishioner *above a certain age,* as Lateran IV had said, nor every man and woman, as 1549 did.

8. See Aidan Kavanagh, *Confirmation: Origins and Reform* (New York: Pueblo, 1988), pp. 1-31.

9. Marion J. Hatchett, *Commentary on the American Prayer Book* (New York: Seabury Press, 1980), pp. 394f.

10. BCP, p. 409.

11. Alcuin Club Collections 47 (London: SPCK, 1965), pp. 101-108.

12. "Infant Communion: Reflections on the Case from Tradition," *Anglican and Episcopal History* 57 (1988): 159-75; reprinted above, pp. 146-64. Her article was in response to C. FitzSimons Allison's earlier article in the same journal, "Anglican Initiatory Rites: A Contribution to the Current Debate," *AEH* 56 (1987): 27-43.

13. See Herman Wegman, *Christian Worship in East and West* (New York: Pueblo, 1985), p. 288.

14. Allison, pp. 37-42 and *passim.*

15. Brightman, *The English Rite,* p. 787.

16. "How many sacraments hath Christ ordained in his Church?" Brightman, p. 787.

17. Mark 7.8.

18. Alexander Schmemann, *Of Water and the Spirit* (New York: St. Vladimir's Seminary Press, 1974), pp. 117ff.

19. Justin Martyr, *First Apology* 65, trans. Edward R. Hardy, in Cyril Richardson, *Early Christian Fathers,* Library of Christian Classics 1 (Philadelphia: Westminster Press, 1953), pp. 285ff.

20. "Letter to Senarius," trans. E. C. Whitaker, *Documents of the Baptismal Liturgy* (London: SPCK, 1970), p. 157.

21. Michel Andrieu, *Ordines Romani,* Vol. 2 (Louvain: Spicilegium Sacrum Lovaniense, 1960), p. 446; trans. Whitaker, p. 204. The rubric survived to appear in the tenth-century Germano-Roman Pontifical, although with an addition permitting the babies to be fed if there is great necessity (*Ordo L* 39.91; Andrieu, vol. 5, p. 295). Many other examples could be cited.

22. St. John Chrysostom, *Baptismal Instructions,* 2.27, trans. Paul W. Harkins, Ancient Christian Writers 31(Westminster, Md.: Newman, 1963), p. 53:

    > Straightway after they have come up from the waters, they are led to the awesome table laden with countless favors, where they taste of the Master's Body and Blood, and become a dwelling place for the Holy Spirit.

23. The Greek text is in Conybeare and Maclean, *Rituale Armenorum* (Oxford: University Press, 1905), p. 406. An English translation appears in Whitaker, *Documents,* p. 82.

24. See Alexander Schmemann, *For the Life of the World: Sacraments and Orthodoxy* (New York: St. Vladimir's Seminary Press, 1973), pp. 76f. See also Casimir Kucharik, *The Byzantine-Slav Liturgy of St. John Chrysostom* (Combermere, Ontario: Alleluia Press, 1971), p. 710:

    > To their credit, all the Orthodox still [administer baptismal communion to infants] faithfully—generally under the form of wine, since infants may not be able to swallow the bread.

25. BCP, p. 298.

26. Allison, p. 37.

28. John Frederick, *The Future of Liturgical Reform* (Wilton, Conn.: Morehouse-Barlow, 1987), pp. 67-70.

29. "And there shall none be admitted to the Holy Communion until such time as he be confirmed, or be ready and desirous to be confirmed" (Book of Common Prayer, 1928, p. 299). "...That children be admitted to Holy Communion before Confirmation, subject to the direction and guidance of the Ordinary...." (Resolution of the 63rd General Convention, Houston, Texas, October 21, 1970, printed in *Services for Trial Use* [New York: Church Hymnal Corporation, 1971], p. 21). "Confirmation should not be regarded as a procedure of admission to the Holy Communion" (the "Pocono Statement" of the House of Bishops, November 1971, in Marion Hatchett, *Commentary on the American Prayer Book,* p. 271).

30. "This regulation in the Church of England goes back to John Peckham, a reform-minded thirteenth century Archbishop of Canterbury who wished to encourage his bishops to do more confirming, a practice they were neglecting. He hoped that by forbidding communion before confirmation he would put pressure on both bishops and parents to bring children to confirmation. Although the regulation has been frequently so used in subsequent centuries, its purpose was neither to exclude Protestants (of whom there were none in the thirteenth century) nor children (since confirmation was then generally administered to infants)" (Leonel L. Mitchell, *Praying Shapes Believing* [Minneapolis: Winston Press, 1985], p. 117).

31. *Doctrina de communione sub utraque specie et parvulorum,* cap. 4, Council of Trent, Session of July 16, 1552, in Heinrich Denzinger, *Enchiridion Symbolorum,* ed. Karl Rahner (Barcelona: Herder, 1957), p. 329; English translation: *The Church Teaches* (St. Louis: Herder, 1955).

32. This resolution did not call for the communion of infants, but did speak of the admission of baptized children to communion

32. This resolution did not call for the communion of infants, but did speak of the admission of baptized children to communion "at an early age after appropriate instruction." It was this resolution which formed the basis for the work of the Drafting Committee on Christian Initiation of the Standing Liturgical Commission of the Episcopal Church, and which resulted in Prayer Book Studies 18 and 26, and the baptismal rite of the American prayer book.

33. New York: Church Pension Fund, 1970.

34. Ibid., p. 40.

35. Ibid., p. 24.

36. *Services for Trial Use,* pp. vi, 21.

37. Issued as a pamphlet for insertion in the service book March 31, 1971.

38. It is, in fact, the abandonment of the Mason-Dix theological position on baptism and confirmation and the reintroduction of a theology of the sufficiency of baptism as "full initiation," a doctrine identified both with the Reformers and patristic theologians, not the approval of infant communion, to which the late Urban Holmes referred as a theological change between 1928 and 1979 ("Education for Liturgy: An Unfinished Symphony in Four Movements," in Malcolm C. Burson, ed., *Worship Points the Way* [New York: Seabury Press, 1981], p. 134).

39. *Holy Baptism, together with A Form for the Affirmation of Baptismal Vows with the Laying-on of Hands by the Bishop, also called Confirmation,* Prayer Book Studies 26 (New York: Church Hymnal Corporation, 1973).

40. Ibid., p. 16.

41. *Supplement to Prayer Book Studies 26* (New York: Church Hymnal Corporation, 1973), pp. 71-7. This material has been revised and republished in Daniel B. Stevick, *Baptismal*

*Moments; Baptismal Meanings* (New York: Church Hymnal Corporation, 1987), pp. 91-114.

42. *Holy Baptism; Authorized for Trial Use during 1975-1976* (New York: Church Hymnal Corporation, 1975), p. 18.

43. New York: Church Hymnal Corporation, 1976.

44. This interpretation was made possible by the removal of the word "now" from the 1975 version of the rubric. This was done because some who accepted Gregory Dix's theology of two-stage initiation were interpreting the rubric in Prayer Book Studies 26 to mean that those baptized "now," i.e., with the rite in PBS 26 containing chrismation with the prayer for the seven gifts of the Spirit, might receive communion, but those baptized in rites, such as that of the (then official) 1928 prayer book, which lacked this ceremony, could not.

45. The text proposed appears in *The Blue Book: Reports of the Committees, Commissions, Boards, and Agencies of the General Convention of the Episcopal Church,* Detroit, Michigan, July 1988, p. 185. The text as adopted is in *The Book of Occasional Services,* Second Edition (and subsequent editions) (New York: Church Hymnal, 1988), p. 157.

46. BCP, p. 860. The requirements are biblical and traditional. They appear also in the exhortation to communion (BCP, p. 316f) and are at root Pauline.

47. BCP, p. 858.

48. Quoted in J. D. C. Fisher, *Christian Initiation: The Reformation Period,* Alcuin Club Collections 51 (London: SPCK, 1970), p. 255.

# 15

# Disputed Aspects of Infant Communion

*Louis Weil*

It is now over two decades since the Episcopal Church at the General Convention of 1970 authorized that children "be admitted to Holy Communion before Confirmation." This authorization, however, did not state whether there should be a specific age at which children should first receive communion, nor did it indicate explicitly whether the intention was that the first reception should be joined with the occasion of the child's baptism.

The result during the intervening years has been a kind of pastoral ambivalence which continues to the present time to produce difficult situations in which children who have received communion since baptism are denied the sacrament when they are visiting at another parish in which some later age is the established practice. These situations where differing expectations come into conflict are painful for the children who are denied the sacrament, and often are occasions of profound anger on the part of their parents. Such incidents should remind us that often we have dealt with this issue at the level of parish policy rather than doing the more difficult work, at both diocesan and national levels, of reflecting on the theological foundations of the issue and attempting thereby to build a wider consensus within the church. The arguments of some who oppose the giving of communion to infants may reflect merely an opposition to change in what they have experienced for a lifetime as the church's practice. But for others, the opposition is based upon firm theological conviction. Both these groups need to be addressed with a respectful understanding of the sources of their opposition if we are to move into a reconciling common ground from which a shared norm may emerge. Our intention here is to look at some of the arguments against the communion of infants from an irenic perspective.

Opponents to the practice of the communion of infants hold that a clear distinction must be made between the church's expectations for baptism and those for the reception of communion. It is asserted that the requirement of faith in infant baptism rests upon the sponsors as representatives of the church. In regard to communion, however, faith is required on the part of the individual communicant. But we must remember that all of the church's expectations in regard to the reception of the sacraments are based upon the normative model of adult believers. *All* of the sacraments presume faith, a faith which finds expression in the mature commitment of adults. This perspective is actually implied in the assertion that infants may be baptized on the basis of the faith of the sponsors in that in such a context there is a derivation of the expectation of faith from the infant candidate to the sponsors. If such derivation is appropriate in the initiatory rites, it is difficult to defend a distinction in regard to the eucharist. If the faith of the sponsors is adequate in the first context, why is it not adequate in the second?

The real issue here is not the proposed theological distinction but rather the realities of pastoral experience. It is comparatively easy for sponsors to be present at a baptism and to repeat the phrases which claim an active faith. It is far more problematic to establish a context in which the professed support of the sponsors will find continuing expression in the life of the child. If we are to administer any sacraments to infants, our pastoral policies in regard to sponsors require transformation in a more thorough preparation of sponsors for what is in fact a very serious responsibility.

Liturgical scholars have often been accused, sometimes for just cause, of a rather naive idealization of the patterns of worship of the early centuries. The suggestion that the primitive unity of baptism, confirmation and communion should be restored has been interpreted as an expression of liturgical archeology, an attempt to impose the pattern of a very different situation upon a culture to which it is not suited. In opposition to this, it has been suggested that the breakdown of the unity of the three elements was in fact providential, and that three separated events are actually better suited to our own complex time. There can be little question that individuals need events over time in which their religious pilgrimage is brought into focus and celebrated in a liturgical form.

Given the wide diversity of our cultural situation, the issue is whether any predetermined pattern can be adjusted to such a complex social reality. In attempting to use the threefold pattern in that way, do we not rather fall between two stools, maintaining a theological muddle which has grown up upon the splintered elements, and yet still not finding a pattern which is appropriate to the pastoral reality? As painful as the debate and confusion over these issues has been, it has been fruitful in forcing us to reexamine the inherited tradition in the light of the theological integrity of the primitive pattern. Dividing up the three facets of incorporation has led only to theological obfuscation. Membership in the Body of Christ is a single reality and can best be signified in a single liturgical reality which encompasses the water rite, the signing, and the sharing of the signs of our participation in the Body and Blood of Christ.

Yet another area of dispute is concerned with the supposed denigration of the importance of instruction which early reception of communion might seem to suggest. We have observed that official statements have affirmed the need for instruction prior to first communion. When infants are communicated at their baptism and thereafter, such preparatory instruction is bypassed, although it is always the intention that such instruction will be given later, when it is suited to the child's level of development.

The matter at issue here draws together a number of considerations. From one perspective, the question is whether rational understanding must precede the reception of God's grace. Surely all would agree that this is not the case. The sacraments all find their source in God's initiative toward us, as is often stated in support of the practice of infant baptism. Bishop FitzSimons Allison has given us a sharp perspective to the issue in showing how balanced an approach is required. He writes, "It is not necessarily superstitious to communicate, for pastoral reasons, infants or those whose consciousness is impaired. But it is likely to evoke superstition when the practice of receiving in ignorance becomes the normal policy of the church."[1] Bishop Allison sees this appropriate concern about superstition as related to a kind of contemporary Apollinarianism in which God's gift of salvation is effective without the cooperation of the human will.

None of us who favor the practice of infant communion would welcome a descent into superstition, but as a missionary priest in Latin America I had ample opportunity to observe how often superstitious attitudes became attached to communion in the lives of adults. Again, the real problem lies beneath the surface of the choice of one pattern or another. It lies in the realm of formation for Christian maturity. If we are to consider infants as in any way the appropriate recipients of sacramental grace, at a time when neither the infant's will nor understanding can be a constitutive factor, then we must look at the professing adult community and be much more concerned than we have been about the deepening of adult understanding and also in helping sponsors to see that the promises which they make at a baptism require a mature will if they are to be carried out. Without such attention to the wider context in which infant baptisms take place, the risk of superstition is great from the first sacramental act.

Our baptismal practice was for centuries deeply affected by a highly individualized understanding of how baptism and salvation are related. Beneath our debates about the various aspects of the initiatory process there lies an even more fundamental question: what does it mean to be a member of the church, the people of God? We are recovering an awareness of the biblical understanding of salvation as God's gift to us as a people, as a community of faith. That recovery offers important insight into baptism and eucharist as mutual signs of our interdependence as God's people. As communities begin to live that corporate understanding of the Christian life, the integral place of children within such communities becomes evident at all levels of the community's life, including the sacramental. In such a context, the unity of all the baptized in the sharing of the eucharistic gifts becomes a powerful sign of God's initiative toward all of us with the gifts of grace and of the mutual interdependence of our lives in receiving them.

## An Ecumenical Perspective

In a study of confirmation, Roman Catholic specialist Gerard Austin has praised the rites of the 1979 Book of Common Prayer, seeing them as an important ecumenical contribution. In regard to the question of the communion of infants, he writes,

> One hopes that this will cause others, including those who are members of other churches, to reexamine the whole question. The new rite implies that the fundamental right to eucharist comes from baptism and not from an extrinsic factor such as the "age of discretion." Any argument against communicating infants could equally argue against infant baptism. Just as in a natural family infants are fed lovingly right from the beginning, so in the church this care should be carried out through the entire process of growth, with the child moving progressively into a deeper understanding of just what is taking place when it is fed at the Lord's Table.[2]

Austin offers us in these words a sensitive perspective to the wider context in which the practice of the communion of infants must be scrutinized. Baptism makes us members of the family of God. In sharing the eucharist, we celebrate that identity.

# Notes

1. C. FitzSimons Allison, "Anglican Initiatory Rites: A Contribution to the Current Debate," *Anglican and Episcopal History* 56 (1987): 37.

2. Gerard Austin, O.P., *Anointing with the Spirit: The Rite of Confirmation* (New York: Pueblo Press, 1985), pp. 76-77. Cf. G. Müller-Fahrenholz, *...and do not hinder them. An ecumenical plea for the admission of children to the eucharist,* Faith and Order Paper 109 (Geneva: World Council of Churches, 1982). For a Lutheran perspective to the question, see Robert W. Jenson, "The Eucharist: for Infants?" *Living Worship,* 15 (1979).

# Appendix 1
## Communion of the Baptized but Unconfirmed

**Report of The Rev. Paul Gibson, Coordinator for Liturgy, to the Joint Meeting of Primates and the Anglican Consultative Council in Cape Town, South Africa, January 1993:**

> Fifteen provinces have reported on this matter. Their responses indicate a very flexible situation in which proposals are being considered and imminent change is possible. Four provinces indicate that the communion of unconfirmed children has been authorized, although there may be variations in practice in some of them. Of the remainder, only four report with a simple negative. The remainder indicate varying degrees of openness and ongoing wrestling with what continues to be a current pastoral challenge. The situation may well have changed at the time of writing.

### Responses as of November 1992*

**Anglican Church of Papua New Guinea**. As of November 1990, this province reports that they are inclined to confirm people younger than most provinces and so have not discussed this issue.

**Church in Wales**. The subject was discussed at the April 1991 meeting of the Governing Body of the Church in the Wales, where it was resolved that (a) the Bench of Bishops establish a working

---

*Editor's Note: Responses from Australia, England, and New Zealand were deleted from this Appendix because the situation in those provinces is discussed elsewhere in this volume.

group to consider the question of baptized children being given communion before confirmation; and (b) that the working group should report its findings to the bishops, recommending, if necessary, appropriate ways in which the questions may be responded to in the Province.

**Church of the Province of Southern Africa.** As of January 1991, admission of children to communion before confirmation was still far from settled in this province, and practice varied from diocese to diocese.

**Province of Tanzania.** The province, through its Liturgical and Faith Committee, considered this issue in May 1989. It was resolved that this province will continue with the present practice of giving communion only to confirmed members. However, it was also left open for review pending more study on the matter.

**Scottish Episcopal Church.** As of February 1991, the seven diocesan bishops in this church have been unable to come to uniform conclusion. For the time being, each bishop has the power to admit to communion baptized but unconfirmed persons that have reached the age of discretion by means of a short service modelled on that of the Province of New Zealand. Some bishops do, others don't. However, the Liturgy Committee, together with the Doctrine and Education Committee of General Synod, are now working on a revision of the initiation rites on the basis of the practice of ECUSA. It is hoped the new revision will be backed by a provincial policy of nurture and education. The only clear point is that anyone admitted to communion anywhere in the Anglican Communion cannot be denied access in any church of the province.

**Episcopal Church of Brazil.** The practice of the direct connection of communion with baptism started in the Diocese of South Central Brazil (S. Paulo) around 1979. Subsequently the practice was introduced in other dioceses. Around 1985 the House of Bishops issued a Pastoral linking baptism to eucharist directly.

**Church of Ireland.** A document was prepared by the House of Bishops in response to discussion and the resolution of Lambeth 1988. The document welcomes the renewed emphasis on baptism which recognizes that the child is already a real member of the church, the emphasis on the church and its renewal, and the difficulties encountered by those responsible for confirmation preparation. However, the House of Bishops is not satisfied that the final word has been said in reappraisal of baptism. Theologically there can be no objection to the admission to communion of those who are baptized. However, the discipline implied by a rubric in the BCP reflects a tradition in scripture (Acts 8) and tradition that there is a place for laying on of hands in the initiatory process which has been challenged but not absolutely refuted. In some cases, bishops are encouraging confirmation at an earlier age. Where the eucharist is established as the weekly service, children may feel excluded; however, although this pattern of worship shows signs of development in Ireland, it is not the prevailing pattern. Personal commitment before communion makes psychological and spiritual sense to children. Confirmation is useful in highlighting personal commitment. The new confirmation liturgy provides for confirmation in the context of holy communion, which is sometimes accompanied by parochial (rather than central) confirmation and first communion. The episcopal role in confirmation emphasizes the link between the bishop and the initiatory process and highlights the importance of what the candidates are undertaking. This link between baptism and confirmation indicates that baptism is not only incorporation into Christ and the church but also begins a process of growth in which confirmation and admission to holy communion are steps. Although the Holy Spirit is given through baptism in water and is known in other ways and occasions, confirmation is to be understood as a special moment of increase in the Holy Spirit. The bishops are not convinced that there should be a change in their practice of confirmation and the discipline surrounding admission to holy communion, although they are aware of problems at the parochial level and have noted the variety of teaching materials and movement from an academic to an experiential approach to preparation.

**Japan (Nippon Sei Ko Kai).** NSKK as a province does not officially permit the communion of the unconfirmed. But in some dioceses, those visitors from other provinces where communion of the unconfirmed is the recognized custom, may be admitted to communion.

This question is still under discussion. It should be noted that there is a tendency for the age of confirmation in recent years to be lowered from fourteen or fifteen to ten and eleven year olds.

**Canada.** Children may be admitted to communion before confirmation, in accordance with diocesan guidelines. There is considerable variety in practice, but those once admitted are not supposed to be refused elsewhere.

**Kenya.** A theological consultation in October 1986 had recommended that children of primary school age and above should be admitted to communion after some basic instruction and a simple ceremony of welcome. They should be admitted only in the company of their parent or guardian who is responsible to ensure that the children receive the sacrament in a proper fashion. The consultation also recommended that ministers plan courses of instruction for parents and for the whole congregation. The service of confirmation should be seen as a commissioning for Christian service and witness and should be administered to young people at about the time of the completion of primary instruction. The consultation called for a draft confirmation service in which the theme of commissioning for service and witness clearly appears.

A second liturgical conference was held 29 April-2 May 1991. It recommended:

> that adult Christians who are baptized should be received immediately to holy communion without waiting for confirmation by the bishop, and that a service of reception to holy communion be conducted by the parish priest;

that children baptized during infancy be given instruction on Christian faith and sacraments during the age of discretion and that a service of reception to holy communion be conducted by the parish priest with the involvement of the whole congregation;

that during the bishop's visit to the parish all those received to holy communion (adults and children) be commissioned by the bishop for their lay ministry in the church and society.

A draft service of commissioning has been prepared but has not yet been approved by the province.

**North India**. The CNI has not taken up for consideration the subject of admitting to communion the baptized but unconfirmed.

**East Asia**. The common practice in the diocese is still communion after confirmation. The diocese has not discussed the theological and pastoral issues involved in the admission of the unconfirmed to communion. On the whole priests and people feel pre-confirmation classes are a great opportunity for the church to teach its faithful before they are admitted to communion. As a church working in a minority situation and surrounded by many other faiths, they must take the teaching opportunity seriously.

# Appendix 2
## Statement of the House of Bishops, General Convention of the Episcopal Church in the U.S.A., July 1988

**Resolution B012a:**

*Whereas*, the Church teaches that Holy Baptism is the sacrament by which God adopts us as children by grace, and makes us, at whatever age we are baptized, members of Christ's Body, the Church; and

*Whereas*, the practice of the church has evolved since previous statements by this House on the subject of communion by young children, so that a statement of the current mind of this House may be useful, now, therefore be it

*Resolved*, that the mind of the House of Bishops is that:

Those baptized in infancy may, as full members of the Body of Christ, begin receiving communion at any time they desire and their parents permit; and that the following pastoral principles are recommended to guide the church in communicating those baptized as infants:

1. That the reception of communion by young children should normally be in the context of their participation with their parents and other family in the liturgy of the church;

2. That instruction is required for adults and older children before their baptism and first communion; instruction is also essential for young children after they are baptized and have received communion in infancy, that they may grow in appre-

ciation of the grace they have received and in their ability to respond in faith, love, and thankful commitment of their lives to God;

3. That pastoral sensitivity is always required: in not forcing the sacrament on an unwilling child, in not rejecting a baptized child who is reaching out for communion with God in Christ, and in respecting the position of the parents of a child in this regard; and

4. That the practice of some parishes which customarily give first communion to infants at their baptism, then next offer them communion when they and their parents express a desire that they receive, is seen to be an acceptable practice in the spirit of these guidelines; and be it further

*Resolved,* that the Committee on Theology be instructed to present a report on this matter to the next House of Bishops meeting.